The Bible Phonics Curriculum

INSTRUCTORS

Activity Workbook
With Readers

Gail Hall, Ed.D.

Fran Brashear-Graphic Designer

Janine Dworin-Artist

Jarrell Comeaux-Composer

TotalRecall Publications, Inc.
1103 Middlecreek
Friendswood, Texas 77546
281-992-3131   281-482-5390 Fax
www.TotalRecallPress.com

All rights reserved. Except as permitted under the United States Copyright Act of 1976, No part of this publication may be reproduced, stored in a retrieval system, or transmitted in any form or by any means electronic or mechanical or by photocopying, recording, or otherwise without prior permission of the publisher. Exclusive worldwide content publication / distribution by TotalRecall Publications, Inc.

Copyright © 2024 by: Gail Hall, Ed.D.
Graphic Designer: Fran Brashear
Artist: Janine Dworin
Composer: Jarrell Comeaux

ISBN: 978-1-64883-080-8
UPC: 6-43977-40808-2

Library of Congress Control Number: 2021935877

FIRST EDITION
1 2 3 4 5 6 7 8 9 10

Judgments as to the suitability of the information herein is the purchaser's responsibility. Mouse Gate Press. extends no warranties, makes no representations, and assumes no responsibility as to the accuracy or suitability of such information for application to the purchaser's intended purposes or for consequences of its use except as described herein.

The scanning, uploading and distribution of this book via the Internet or via any other means without the permission of the publisher is illegal and punishable by law. Please purchase only authorized electronic editions, and do not participate in or encourage electronic piracy of copyrighted materials. Your support of the author's rights is appreciated.

To the Glory and Honor of the Almighty God
To my Carverdale family
To Jaysen and Caleb
To Children Everywhere

Foreword

Dr. Gail Hall was my first Bible school teacher and spiritual mentor. Under her tutelage, I was able to view the written word of God through both a spiritual and intellectual lens. She always insisted that in order to develop a personal relationship with God, it was essential that her students have the ability to "read the words on the page."

This Bible Phonics Curriculum is a merging of her evangelistic nature and professional acumen. In this age of information, it is not enough to tell our children that God is real, we must capture them at their most inquisitive and ignite in them the passion that led the Bereans to "search the scriptures daily," (Acts 17:11).

I am of the firm belief that this work will prove to be a fun, and intellectual exercise for both student and teacher, for as the Proverb writer said, "the fear of the Lord is the beginning of knowledge…" (Proverbs 1:7).

--Coiette Gaston, Ed. D.

The Bible Phonics Curriculum

The goal of the Bible Phonics Curriculum is to restore and commit to teach reading integrated with Bible stories. The objective of each lesson seeks to inure some altruistic learning along with the alphabetic principle. The stories, the readers, and workbook activities are student centered. The hope is that any who would indulge would not only become familiar with phonemic awareness but will after experiencing the wonderment of God's word seek to make their life better.

The curriculum can be most helpful to you if you follow and abide by the guidelines in the instructional manual. This instructional tool will aid you in using this curriculum and achieving amazing results.

One of the components of the curriculum is that it is systematic, structured, and organized. The structure of the Bible lessons help to minimize teacher preparation. It is systematic in that the Bible lessons are easy to comprehend and to follow sequentially. The Bible lessons are also organized based on Bible people in ABC order. This will help enhance student's recognition and articulation of the basic sounds in the alphabet. This will provide an opportunity for you, the instructor, to facilitate and assess student learning. Your students can spend time enjoying learning.

Emily Calhoun's (1998) Picture Word Index Model helps the student to identify all familiar words in a picture. This process is also called "shaking out words".

The teacher then acts as a scribe by simply drawing a line from the visual image to chart paper or a whiteboard.

The teacher spells orally the words with students daily. This enhances children's listening, speaking and writing vocabularies.

The teacher and students begin to make sentences using the words shared by the students.

After rehearsing the story four (4) times, the students can be scaffolded towards writing or dictating a story reviewing the beginning, middle, and end of each Bible story.

The teacher should utilize the Phonics song and Name song to help students become familiar with each letter's sound. By so doing, the teacher creates the environment for each student to become a Reader. The other benefit is that those hidden curricula build Christian attributes and citizenry that are being embodied subconsciously in the minds of each student.

Things to Note:

Each lesson can be divided into days or weeks. The objective is to celebrate each letter for a month. These lessons can be utilized in a Bible curriculum-based school, church, homeschool environment or devotional setting. Note that days or weeks 1, 2, 3, and 4 can be rehearsed the same for each letter. Note this for the letter A. Follow this pattern for all of the letters.

Day 1/Week 1
The teacher will introduce the alphabet of the month and the Bible character of the month.
The teacher will allow students (preschool and school aged) to shake out words from the visual image provided.
The teacher will write the words by drawing a line from the image to chart paper or whiteboard.
The teacher will rehearse the words and spell them aloud with the class.
The teacher will then read the lesson as scripted on the opposite side of the picture or page.

Day 2/Week 2
The teacher and students will shake out a few more words from the visual image provided and then reread the story from Day 1/Week 1.
The teacher will draw a line from the picture and write the words shared by the class.
The teacher will begin to make sentences from the words.

Review the Bible verse using the paper sentence strips.

Bible Verse: "In the beginning, God created the heavens and the earth" (Genesis 1:01).
Word Wall Words – Adam, apple, Bible, Genesis

Day 3/Week 3
The teacher will read the story from Day 1/Week 1.
The teacher will ask the class to share words that begin with the letter Aa or the letter of the month.
The teacher and students will write some more sentences about the story and the Word Wall words.

The teacher will write the words given by the class to begin the Word Wall
Adam, apple, at, etc.…

Review the Bible verse using the paper sentence strips.

Day 4/Week 4
The teacher will read the story from Day 1/Week 1.
The teacher will review the Word Wall Words.
The teacher will assist the students writing or dictating the beginning, middle, and end of the Bible story.

Review Bible verse using the paper sentence strips.
The teacher and students will make as many sentences as possible about the Bible story.
The teacher will review the Plan of Salvation Rap each time the class meets.

After each lesson, the teacher should plan for center or station activities.
Suggestions for Center Activities or Stations: Puzzles, review of the alphabet and numbers, sorting colors and shapes, rehearsing familiar sounds, creating patterns with word tiles, and sight words. Activity Workbook pages and readers for each lesson are also provided.

Tidbits for Users of The Bible Phonics Curriculum

Follow the scripted lessons, and remember Teachers, Take your Time. These lessons were created for a month-long study or two depending on how fast or frequently you meet with your students. The lessons are structured, systematic, and organized so that your prep time is diminished and you can focus on assessing your students in whole group and small group environments.

Word Wall Words are suggested throughout the curriculum. You may create your own words. Words provided by the students will drive this activity.

Create and decorate an Attendance Chart for your students. The students will enjoy seeing their names highlighted on the Attendance Chart.

Decorate your teaching area with student work.

Use the Sentence Strip provided in the Workbook for recreating the Bible verses for each lesson. Allow the students who can write to copy and decorate the sentence strips for the class. Cut them up and use them in a center activity.

Invest in Centers or Stations by creating or buying sets of numbers, alphabets, word tiles, math facts, or sight word puzzles.

Teachers, it may take more than two sessions to actually teach the story. Some stories are a little more complex to understand. The vocabulary is a little more challenging for some age groups. It may take you a little longer to work through the vocabulary. This is a good thing. Do not be alarmed. This only makes the learning more concrete.

As time allots, let the students guess when introducing a new consonant if the tongue, teeth, or lips block that particular sound. The same for a name that begins with a vowel, let students determine if the sound says its name or is a short sound.

Tidbits for Users of The Bible Phonics Alphabet Readers

Rehearse the sounds of the alphabet before studying each lesson.

For preschool students, the teacher will read the individual readers to them. Encourage the parents and family members to read the Bible stories to their children.

For students in kindergarten or in an early primary grade, the readers can be utilized in small group reading sessions. The small group sessions can focus on defining words that students do not understand, then reading practice focusing on fluency and comprehension. The readers can also be sent home for the student to practice with family members.

Teachers, feel free to connect and teach any word patterns such as the same beginning or ending sounds (rhyming) or any phonic connections to help students decode difficult words.

Teachers use the underlined words in a choral read session as you read to your students. In other words, allow students to shout out the words with you as you read to them during whole and small group.

Tidbits for Users of the The Bible Phonic Workbook

Teachers feel free to use the workbook activities to supplement the lesson. Lessons will not be long and this will provide tactile kinesthetic learning for all of your students.

Plan of Salvation Rap

Let's review the steps that you take to become a member of the Church:
You hear God's word and believe it in your heart,
Everyone points to their ears and head.

You confess with your mouth that Jesus is Lord,
Everyone points to their lips.

You repent of your sins and say NO MORE,
Everyone shakes their heads "NO".

And are baptized into Christ to live with God Evermore!
Everyone put hands together and move to the left to symbolize being baptized and bring hands back up to symbolize becoming a New Creation.

Hear-Romans 10:17
Believe-Hebrews 11:06
Repent-Acts 17:30
Confession-Romans 10:09-10
Baptism-Acts 2:38

LESSONS

Lesson 1/Day 1-The Letter A

<u>Text: Genesis 1</u>

Teacher: Hello Boys and Girls,

I am so happy that you are in Bible Class (today or tonight). Thank you for being here. We are going to celebrate the letter Aa. The letter Aa is a vowel. Vowels can make a long or short sound. This letter Aa in this story is a short sound. (Today or tonight) we will learn the short sound that the letter Aa makes. Repeat the sound with me please -Aa, Aa, Adam. Aa, Aa, Adam.

We will study about a person in the Bible whose name began with a short A. His name was Adam. Repeat it with me please -Aa, Aa, Adam. Aa, Aa, Adam. Adam was the first man that God created. God created Adam on the sixth day of the beginning of the world. He made Adam out of the dust of the ground. Isn't that great? No one can create another human being.

We can find the story of Adam in the book of Genesis, the first chapter. This is the first book in the Old Testament and the first book in the Bible. Before God created Adam, he made the sky, vegetables, plants, trees, lights, sun, moon, animals and all living creatures. God was very busy creating a beautiful world for us to live in. Don't you want to help others keep God's world beautiful?

Bible Verse: "In the beginning, God created the heavens and the earth" (Genesis 1:01).

Teacher: Let me ask you some questions.
- Q: Who did God create on the sixth day?
- *A: Man or Adam*
- Q: Can you name some other things that God created?
- *A: Sun, moon, etc.*
- Q: Why do you think God made such a beautiful world for us to live in?
- *A: I think God made such a beautiful world for us to live in because he loves us.*
- Q: Name the first book in the Bible.
- *A: Genesis*

Teacher: Ask students if they have any questions.
- Refer to Activity Workbook Lesson 1
- Word Wall Words: Adam, apple, Bible, Genesis,...

B
is for Baal

Lesson 2/Day 1-The Letter B

Text: 1 Kings 18

Teacher: Hello Boys and Girls,

I am so happy that you are in Bible Class (today or tonight). Thank you for being here. We are going to celebrate the letter Bb. The letter Bb is what we call a consonant. Consonants are sounds that close the mouth. The sound is blocked by the tongue, teeth, or lips. (Today or tonight) we will learn the sound that the letter Bb makes. Repeat the sound with me please -Bb, Bb, Baal (Bell). Bb, Bb, Baal (Bell).

We will learn and know that God talks to us through the Bible. The story that we will study comes from the book of I Kings, chapter 18. I Kings is the eleventh book in the Bible. I Kings is the eleventh book in the Old Testament.

In this chapter is the story of God's prophet Elijah. Elijah challenged the prophets of Baal. In this account, Elijah told King Ahab that the living God was greater than their god Baal. Ahab took the challenge. There were 450 prophets against Elijah that day on Mount Carmel.

They sacrificed two bulls, one for the false prophets and the other for the true and living God. God sent fire and burned up "the sacrifice, wood, the stones, and the soil, and also licked up the water in the trench" I Kings 18:38.

The prophets of Baal called on their god from morning until evening, but their god did not answer them. God answered Elijah's call and showed the people of Israel that there was only One true and living God. We can always count on God to hear and answer our prayers because he loves and cares for us.

*Denote the difference between the big G in God and the little g in god.

Bible Verse: "If you believe, you will receive whatever you ask for in prayer" (Matthew 21:22).

Teacher: Let me ask you some questions:
- Q: Where is this story about Baal found in the Bible?
- *A: This story about Baal is found in I Kings 18.*
- Q: Who is the prophet who stands with God?
- *A: The prophet who stands with God is named Elijah.*
- Q: How many prophets of Baal did not believe in the One True God?
- *A: Four-hundred and fifty (450) prophets believed in their god Baal instead of the One True God.*
- Q: Can we believe and trust that God will hear and answer our prayers?
- *A: We can believe and trust that God will hear and answer our prayers.*
- Q: Has God ever answered your prayers before?
- *A: Answers will vary.*

Teacher: Ask students if they have any questions.
Refer to Activity Workbook Lesson 2
Word Wall Words: Baal, book,...

C is for Cain

Lesson 3/Day 1-The Letter C

Text: Genesis 4:1-10

Teacher: Hello Boys and Girls,

I am so happy that you are in Bible Class (today or tonight). Thank you for being here. We are going to celebrate the letter Cc. The letter Cc is what we call a consonant. Consonants are sounds that close the mouth. The sound is blocked by the tongue, teeth, or lips. (Today or tonight) we will learn the sound that the letter Cc makes. Repeat the sound with me please -Cc, Cc, Cain.

We will learn and know that God talks to us through the Bible. The Bible is the Word of God. Isn't it wonderful that not only did God create or make us, he wrote a book to us and taught us about the first family, too. We must learn how to read and appreciate and obey the words in God's book called the what?

Class response... *The* Bible. This story comes from the book of Genesis, the first book in the Bible.

In the first family, there were problems. It was time to make an offering to God. An offering is something that we give to God to show God how much we love him. Abel made an acceptable offering (means that God was pleased) and Cain did not. Cain got so angry that he killed his brother. That made God sad. Should we ever get that angry? God sent Cain away for what he had done. He was very sad that Cain had sinned against Him and against his brother.

Bible Verse: "He that loveth not knoweth not God; for God is love" (I John 4:08).

Teacher: Let me ask you some questions:
- Q: Name the first brothers.
- A: *Cain and Abel*
- Q: What did they have to do?
- A: *They had to give an offering to the Lord.*
- Q: What is an offering?
- A: *An offering is something that you give to God to show God how much you love him.*
- Q: Why did Cain get angry with his brother?
- A: *Cain got angry with his brother because God accepted Abel's offering and not his offering.*
- Q: Do you think it is good to get angry with your brothers and sisters?
- A: *Answers will vary.*

Teacher: Ask students if they have any questions.
Refer to Activity Workbook Lesson 3
Word Wall Words: Cain, cat,...

Lesson 4/Day 1-The Letter D

Text-Genesis 3:1-6

Teacher: Hello Boys and Girls,

I am so happy that you are in Bible Class (today or tonight). Thank you for being here. We are going to celebrate the letter Dd. The letter Dd is what we call a consonant. Consonants are sounds that close the mouth. The sound is blocked by the tongue, teeth, or lips. (Today or tonight) we will learn the sound that the letter Dd makes. Repeat the sound with me please -Dd, Dd, Devil. Dd, Dd, Devil.

We will learn and know that the Devil tries to get us to do things against God. The Bible is the Word of God. Isn't it wonderful that not only did God create and make us, He wrote a book to teach us to only listen to Him, not the devil. We must learn how to read, appreciate and obey the words in God's book called the what?

Class response… *The Bible.* Today's story comes from the book of Genesis, the first book in the Bible.

With the first man (Adam) and woman (Eve), God had given them instructions. Instructions are things that we need to do. God created a beautiful garden full of delicious fruit, but there was one tree that they could not eat from. Adam and Eve were not to eat from the tree that was in the middle of the garden.

The devil talked Eve first into eating from the tree that God told them not to eat from. Then Eve gave her husband fruit from the tree and he ate it also. God told them that if they ate from that tree, they would die. In Genesis 3:4, the devil said, "You will not surely die." That is not what God told them to do. Because of their disobedience, Adam and Eve were disciplined or punished by God.

Although God had to teach Adam and Eve a lesson, he still loved them. Sometimes, when our parents have to discipline us, they still love us and want us to learn to obey and do better.

Wouldn't you rather please God than make Him sad? I would. Let's review our Bible verse.

Bible Verse: "We ought to obey God rather than men" (Acts 5:29).

Teacher: Let me ask you some questions:
- Q: Name the man and the woman in this story.
- *A: Adam and Eve*
- Q: What were they not supposed to do?
- *A: They were not to eat of the tree in the middle of the Garden of Eden.*
- Q: What happened when the serpent came and spoke to Eve?
- *A: The serpent told Eve that it if she ate from the tree in the middle of the garden, she would **not** die.*
- Q: Why do you think that Eve decided to go ahead and disobey God?
- *A: Answers will vary.*
- Q: Do you sometimes disobey God when you know that it is wrong to do?
- *A: Answers will vary.*

Teacher: Ask students if they have any questions.
Refer to Activity Workbook Lesson 4
Word Wall Words: Devil, dog,…

Lesson 5/Day 1-The Letter E

Text-Genesis 5:21-24

Teacher: Hello Boys and Girls,

I am so happy that you are in Bible Class (today or tonight). Thank you for being here. We are going to celebrate the letter Ee. The letter Ee is what we call a vowel. Vowels can make a long or short sound. This letter Ee in this story is a long sound. (Today or tonight) we will learn the sound that the letter Ee makes. Repeat the sound with me please -Ee, Ee, Enoch. Ee, Ee, Enoch. The Ee says its name.

We will learn and know that the Enoch walked with God. Repeat it with me please Ee, Ee, Enoch- Ee, Ee, Enoch.

Q: Where can we find this story about Enoch?
A: Class response... *The Bible.*

Today's story comes from the book of Genesis, the first book in the Bible.

The Bible contains all the wonderful things that God wanted to share with us so that we would make the choice to always follow Him. In our lesson text, the Bible tells us that Enoch walked with God. He did not die, for God took him. His father, Jared, died at the age of 962. His son, Methuselah, died at the age of 969. God took Enoch with him when he was 365 years old.

Q: What does that make you think about the type of person Enoch might have been?
A: *Answers will vary*
   He must have been very special to God because Genesis 5:23 says,
   "And Enoch walked with God."
Q: Do you want to follow God and always be obedient to Him?
A: *Answers will vary*
Q: How can we walk with God?
A: *Answers will vary*
Q: How can we be obedient to God?
A: *Answers will vary*

We should always want to obey God because He loves us so Much. Let's review our Bible verse.

Bible Verse: "For God so loved the world, that he gave his only begotten Son. And whosoever believeth in Him should not perish but have everlasting life" (John 3:16).

Teacher: Let me ask you some questions:
   Q: How old was Enoch when God took him?
   A: *Enoch was three-hundred sixty-five years old (365) when God took him.*
   Q: How old was his father, Jared, when he died?
   A: *Jared was nine-hundred sixty-two years old (962) when he died.*
   Q: How old was his son, Methuselah, when he died?
   A: *Methuselah was nine-hundred sixty-nine years old (969) when he died.*
   Q: Why do you think that God took Enoch with Him?
   A: *Answers will vary*

Teacher: Ask students if they have any questions.
   Activities: Refer to Activity Workbook Lesson 5
   Word Wall Words: Enoch, eat,...

F
is for Festus

Lesson 6/Day 1-The Letter F

Text-Acts 25:21-24

Teacher: Hello Boys and Girls,

I am so happy that you are in Bible Class (today or tonight). Thank you for being here. We are going to celebrate the letter Ff. The letter Ff is what is called a consonant.

Consonants are sounds that close the mouth. The sound is blocked by the tongue, teeth, or lips. (Today or tonight) we will learn the sound that the letter Ff makes. Repeat the sound with me please -Ff, Ff, Festus. Ff, Ff, Festus.

We will learn and know that Festus was the Roman government official who took Paul to meet with King Agrippa. Repeat it with me please Ff, Ff, Festus-Ff, Ff, Festus.

Q: Where can we find this story about Festus?
A: Class response... *The Bible, Acts 25.*

Today's story comes from the book of Acts, the fifth book in the New Testament. In the book of Acts are the actual *acts* of the church in its infancy or beginning. The name of the book "Acts" refers to the *acts* (verb) of the church (what the people did) in the beginning of the church.

In Acts 25, Festus was an official of the Roman government. He had the authority to bring a case against Paul if the evidence supported it. This means that Paul could have gotten in trouble with the government. But it was God working through Festus to allow Paul to speak about God and share how God changed his life. God did not allow the Jewish leaders to take Paul to Jerusalem where they were planning to kill him.

It does not matter who decides to say something bad about you or try to say you did something wrong, God can and will always take care of you (I Peter 5: 07). This verse says, "Cast all your cares on HIM, for He cares for you". The Jewish leaders wanted to say bad things about Paul and even kill him, but God used Festus to help him share about how good God had been to him.

We should always want to walk and obey God because He loves us so Much. Let's review our Bible verse.

Bible Verse: "Cast all your cares on HIM, for He cares for you" (1Peter 5:07).

Teacher: Let me ask you some questions.
Q: Who was Festus?
A: *Festus was a government official.*
Q: Do you want to follow God and always be obedient to Him?
A: *Answers will vary. I want to follow God and always obey Him because...*
Q: Did Festus let the Jewish leaders take Paul to Jerusalem?
A: *No, he did not allow the Jewish leaders to take Paul to Jerusalem.*
Q: How can we be obedient to God?
A: *Answers will vary. We can be obedient to God by...*

Teacher: Ask students if they have any questions.
Activities: Refer to Activity Workbook, Lesson 6
Word Wall Words: Festus, food, ...

Lesson 7/Day 1-The Letter G

<u>Text-1 Samuel 17</u>

Teacher: Hello Boys and Girls,

I am so happy that you are in Bible Class (today or tonight). Thank you for being here. We are going to celebrate the letter Gg. The letter Gg is what is called a consonant. Who remembers what a consonant is? Consonants are sounds that close the mouth. The sound is blocked by the tongue, teeth, or lips. (Today or tonight) we will learn the sound that the letter Gg makes. Repeat the sound with me please -Gg, Gg, Goliath. Gg, Gg, Goliath.

Repeat it with me please Gg, Gg, Goliath-Gg, Gg, Goliath.

Q: Where can we find this story about Goliath?
A: Class response… *The Bible, 1 Samuel 17.*

Today's story comes from the book of 1Samuel, a book in the Old Testament. In the book of 1 Samuel chapter 17, God's people are being teased or made fun of by the Philistine army. Jesse, David's father, had three sons who fought with Israel (the army of God). Jesse sent David to take them food and to check on them. While David was doing that, he saw Goliath tease the armies of God. Now Goliath was a giant (bigger than normal men), he stood nine feet tall. He also wore lots of armor to protect himself. Everyday he would tease the armies of God saying to Israel to send someone down to fight him.

David was the youngest of Jesse's sons but David was a strong and brave young shepherd. David took care of the family's sheep. He had destroyed a bear and a lion with the help of God because those animals had attacked his sheep. After David said what he could do to Goliath, Saul sent David to fight him. I don't know if Saul believed David or not but Goliath mocked or made fun of David when he saw that he was just a young teenage boy.

David faced Goliath and told him that he would kill him with the help of God. That is exactly what happened. David killed Goliath with a sling and a smooth stone. God was with David and he defeated the enemy of God. Just like God defeated Goliath with a sling and a smooth stone, God will defeat any enemy that tries to divide God's people.

Bible Verse: "I can do all things through Christ who strengthens me" (Philippians 4:13).

Teacher: Let me ask you some questions.
Q: Who was Goliath?
A: A giant who wanted to defeat the army of God.
Q: How big was Goliath?
A: Goliath was nine (9) feet tall.
Q: What was he trying to do?
A: He was trying to scare the Israelites. He wanted them to send someone to fight him.
Q: Who decided to go against the giant (Goliath)?
A: David, the shepherd boy.
Q: How did he fight Goliath? What did he have?
A: He fought the giant Goliath with a sling and smooth stone.

Teacher: Ask students if they have any questions.
Activities: Refer to Activity Workbook, Lesson 7
Word Wall Words: Goliath, good,…

H
is for Hagar

Lesson 8/Day 1-The Letter H

Text-Genesis 16

Teacher: Hello Boys and Girls,

I am so happy that you are in Bible Class (today or tonight). Thank you for being here. We are going to celebrate the letter Hh. The letter Hh is what is called a consonant. Who remembers what a consonant is? Consonants are sounds that close the mouth. The sound is blocked by the tongue, teeth, or lips. We will learn the sound that the letter Hh makes. Repeat the sound with me please -Hh, Hh, Hagar. Hh, Hh, Hagar.

Q: Where can we find this story about Hagar?
A: Class response… *The Bible, Genesis 16.*

Today's story comes from the book of Genesis, the first book in the Bible, the first book in the Old Testament. In Genesis 16, Sarai (Abraham's wife) had not had any children. God had promised that Abraham would have a Big family. The Bible says that Abraham believed God (Genesis 15:06).

But Sarai still had not had any children. She decided to help God. Students, God does not need any help from us. God only needs us to be obedient. Sarai had a handmaiden or a servant girl named Hagar. Since she had not had any children, she told her husband to have a child with Hagar. Abraham did as his wife asked of him.

When Hagar became pregnant, she despised Sarai because she could not have children. Sarai mistreated Hagar and Hagar took Ishmael (her son) and ran away. God sent an angel to bring Hagar and Ishmael back home. When Hagar encountered the angel of God, she said, "I have now seen the One who sees me." (Genesis 16:13). God promised that Hagar's son would be a mighty nation. Abram was eighty-six (86) years old when his son with Hagar named Ishmael was born. Remember class, God sees you. His eyes see everything that we do. Let's learn our Bible verse.

Bible Verse: "I have now seen the One who sees me" (Genesis 16:13).

Teacher: Let me ask you some questions.
Q: Who was Sarai?
A: Abraham's wife.
Q: Who was Hagar?
A: She was the handmaiden or servant girl of Sarai.
Q: Why did Sarai suggest that Abraham and Hagar have a child?
A: Sarai suggested that Abraham and Hagar have a child because she did not believe God. She did not know how God would give Abraham a Big family.
Q: What was the name of the son of Abraham and Hagar?
A: The name of the son of Abraham and Hagar was Ishmael.
Q: What did Sarai do after the birth of Ishmael?
A: She told Abraham to send Hagar and Ishmael away. But God sent an angel to bring Hagar and Ishmael back home.

Teacher: Ask students if they have any questions.
Activities: Refer to Activity Workbook, Lesson 8
Word Wall Words: Hagar, help,…

I is for Isaac

Lesson 9/Day 1-The Letter I

<u>Text-Genesis 21-22</u>

Teacher: Hello Boys and Girls,

I am so happy that you are in Bible Class (today or tonight). Thank you for being here. Today we are going to celebrate the letter Ii. The letter Ii is what is called a vowel. Vowels can make a long or short sound. (Today or tonight) we will learn the sound that the letter Ii makes. For this lesson, this Ii sound makes a long vowel sound. Repeat the sound with me please -Ii, Ii, Isaac. Ii, Ii, Isaac.

Today, we will learn who Isaac was. Repeat it with me please Ii, Ii, Isaac-Ii, Ii, Isaac.

Q: Where can we find this story about Isaac?
A: Class response… <u>*The Bible, The book of Genesis.*</u>

Today's story comes from the book of Genesis, the first book in the Bible, the first book in the Old Testament. In Genesis 21, Sarah (Abraham's wife) had not had any children. God had promised that Abraham would have a Big family. The Bible says that Abraham believed God (Genesis 15: 06).

Sarah (Genesis 22) became pregnant after a long time and had a son. When Sarah had a son, Abraham named him Isaac. Abraham was a hundred (100) years old when Isaac was born. He was the son that God had promised Abraham and Sarah.

God tested Abraham by telling Abraham to sacrifice or kill his only son as a burnt offering. Abraham obeyed God. Before he was to sacrifice Isaac on the altar, God provided a ram and Abraham did not have to offer his only son as a burnt offering to God. God knew then that Abraham trusted and believed God.

Bible Verse: "Trust in the Lord with all your heart" (Proverbs 3: 05a).

Teacher: Let me ask you some questions.
    Q: Who was Abraham and Sarah's son?
    A: Abraham and Sarah's son was named Isaac.
    Q: How old was Abraham when Isaac was born?
    A: Abraham was a hundred (100) years old when Isaac was born.
    Q: What did God tell Abraham to do?
    A: God told Abraham to offer his only son Isaac as a sacrifice to him.
    Q: What did Abraham do?
    A: Abraham obeyed God. But Abraham did not have to offer Isaac. God provided a ram instead.
    Q: Did Abraham show that he trusted and believed God?
    A: Abraham did show how much he trusted and believed God because he was willing to sacrifice his only son.
    Q: How much should we trust God?
    A: We should trust God with our very lives. Answers will vary.

Teacher: Ask students if they have any questions.
    Activities: Refer to Activity Workbook, Lesson 9
    Word Wall Words: Isaac, ice, iron,…

J
is for Jacob

Lesson 10/Day 1-The Letter J

Text-Genesis 25 and 27

Teacher: Hello Boys and Girls,

I am so happy that you are in Bible Class (today or tonight). Thank you for being here. Today we are going to celebrate the letter Jj. The letter Jj is what is called a consonant.

Who remembers what a consonant is? Consonants are sounds that close the mouth. The sound is blocked by the tongue, teeth, or lips. (Today or tonight) we will learn the sound that the letter Jj makes. Repeat the sound with me please -Jj, Jj, Jacob. Jj, Jj, Jacob.

Q: Where can we find the story about Jacob?
A: Class response… *The Bible, The book of Genesis.*

Today's story comes from the book of Genesis, the first book in the Bible, the first book in the Old Testament. In Genesis 25 and Genesis 27, the Bible talks about Jacob and his family. Jacob father's name was Isaac. If you remember, Isaac is the son of Abraham and Sarah. Isaac grows up and marries a woman named Rebekah. Isaac and Rebekah have twin sons, named Esau and Jacob. Esau's skin was hairy, whereas, Jacob's skin was smooth (Gen. 27:11). Esau sold his birthright for food, but while Rebekah was pregnant, it was prophesied that the oldest son would serve the younger son (Gen. 25:25). God wanted Jesus to come through the family line of Jacob and God set his plan in action. Remember, we are not as smart as God. God always knows how to make his plans work.

Bible Verse: "For my thoughts are not your thoughts, neither are your ways my ways" (Isaiah: 55:08).

Teacher: Let me ask you some questions.
Q: What was Jacob's brother name?
A: Jacob's brother's name was Esau.
Q: What was different about Jacob and Esau?
A: *Jacob's skin was smooth and Esau's skin was hairy.*
Q: What did Jacob do to his brother?
A: *Jacob tricked Esau out of his birthright and blessing.*
Q: Do you think that God has a plan for all of us to be saved?
A: *I believe and know that God has a plan for all of us to be saved.*
Q: Can we ever be as smart as God?
A: *We can never be as smart as God. We must trust God for our salvation.*

Teacher: Ask students if they have any questions.
Activities: Refer to Activity Workbook, Lesson 10
Word Wall Words: Jacob, jar, jelly,…

K
is for Kenites

Lesson 11/Day 1-The Letter K

<u>Text-Judges 1:16; 1 Samuel 15:6</u>

Teacher: Hello Boys and Girls,

    I am so happy that you are in Bible Class (today or tonight). Thank you for being here. Today we are going to celebrate the letter Kk. The letter Kk is what is called a consonant.

    Q: Who remembers what a consonant is? Consonants are sounds that close the mouth. The sound is blocked by the tongue, teeth, or lips. (Today or tonight) we will learn the sound that the letter Kk makes. Repeat the sound with me please -Kk, Kk, Kenites. Kk, Kk, Kenites.

    Q: Where can we find the story about the Kenite people?

    A: Class response... <u>The Bible, Books in the Old Testament-Genesis, Exodus,... Numbers, Judges,... and I Samuel.</u>

    Today's story comes from the book of Judges, the seventh book in the Bible, the seventh book in the Old Testament. In Judges 1:16, the Bible states that Moses' father-in-law, Jethro, was a Kenite. Jethro was a shepherd and priest who lived in the land of Midian. The Kenites journeyed with the Israelites to the land of Canaan. The Kenites also showed kindness to the Israelites when they came out of Egypt (I Samuel 15:6). King Saul did not want to destroy the Kenites with the Amalekites who lived in the city of Amalek. Historically, the Kenites were nomadic, meaning that they traveled around. They were also attributed with the invention of working with bronze, iron, playing musical instruments, and creating art. The Kenites also were a part of God's plan through Moses. We are also a part of God's plan. We should learn to follow God's plan just the way that God tells us to.

Bible Verse: "Be kind and compassionate to one another, forgiving each other, just as in Christ God forgave you" (Ephesians 4:32).

Teacher: Let me ask you some questions.
    Q: Name one well known Kenite?
    A: One well known Kenite was Moses' father-in-law, Jethro.
    Q: Name one thing the Kenite people are known for.
    A: One thing the Kenite people are known for is working with bronze and iron.
       Answers may vary.
    Q: How were the Kenites a part of God's plan?
    A: The Kenites were a part of God's plan because they showed kindness to the Israelites when they came out of Egypt.
    Q: Should we be kind to each other? Give examples.
    A: We should be kind to each other. Answers will vary.

Teacher: Ask students if they have any questions.
    Activities: Refer to Activity Workbook, Lesson 11
    Word Wall Words: Kenites, kite, kitten,...

L
is for Lazarus

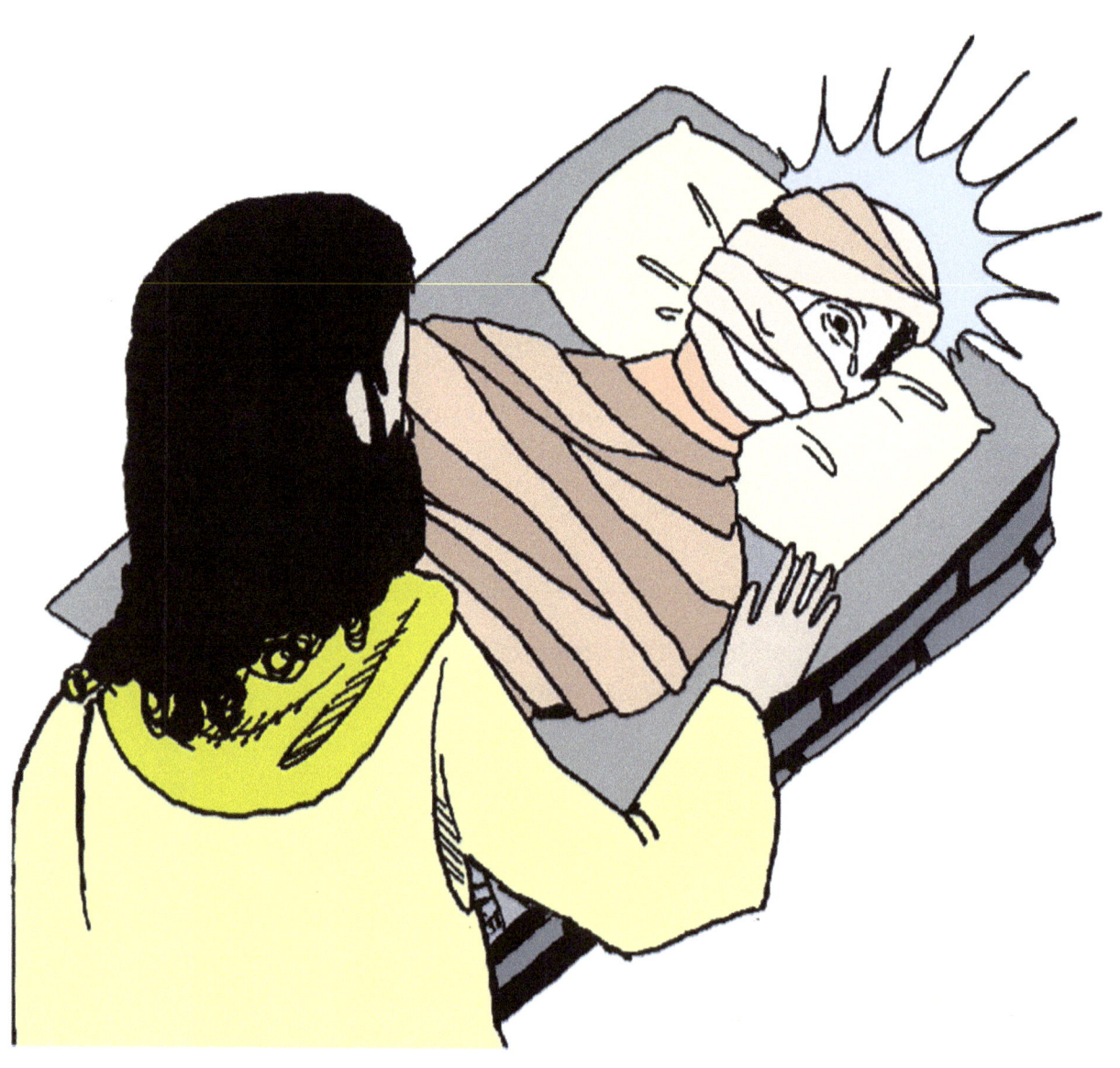

Lesson 12/Day 1-The Letter L

Text-John 11:1-46

Teacher: Hello Boys and Girls,

I am so happy that you are in Bible Class (today or tonight). Thank you for being here. We are going to celebrate the letter Ll. The letter Ll is what is called a consonant.

Who remembers what a consonant is? Consonants are sounds that close the mouth. The sound is blocked by the tongue, teeth, or lips. (Today or tonight) we will learn the sound that the letter Ll makes. Repeat the sound with me please -Ll, Ll, Lazarus. Ll, Ll, Lazarus.

Q: Where can we find the story of Lazarus?
A: Class response… *The Bible, Books in the New Testament-Matthew, Mark, Luke and John.*

Today's story comes from the book of John, the fourth book in the New Testament. In John 11:1-46, we read about the raising of Lazarus from the dead. Lazarus had two sisters, Mary and Martha. They were all close friends to Jesus. Imagine that, being close friends to Jesus. They were the kind of friends that could sit down and eat together and hang out together. I hope that you consider Jesus a friend that you can take anywhere. Back to our story, in the book of John, Mary and Martha's brother Lazarus got real sick and he died. He died and was buried four (4) days before Jesus got back to Bethany where he lived. Yes, Mary and Martha were very sad because their brother died. Can you guess what happened? Jesus brought Lazarus back to life. God is Able to do whatever we believe that he can do.

Bible Verse: "I am the resurrection and the life" (John 11:23).

Teacher: Let me ask you some questions.
Q: Where is this story found in the Bible?
A: This story is found in the book of John 11:1-46.
Q: What are the names of Jesus' friends?
A: The names of Jesus' friends are Mary, Martha, and Lazarus.
Q: Who was sick and died?
A: Lazarus became very ill and died.
Q: How long was Lazarus dead before Jesus reached him?
A: Lazarus had been dead four days before Jesus brought him back to life.
Q: How do think Mary and Martha felt after Jesus raised Lazarus from the dead?
A: Answers will vary.

Teacher: Ask students if they have any questions.
Activities: Refer to Activity Workbook, Lesson 12
Word Wall Words: Lazarus, lion, little,…

M
is for Moses

Lesson 13/Day 1-The Letter M

<u>Text-Exodus 2:1-10</u>

Teacher: Hello Boys and Girls,

I am so happy that you are in Bible Class (today or tonight). Thank you for being here. We are going to celebrate the letter Mm. The letter Mm is what is called a consonant.

Who remembers what a consonant is? Consonants are sounds that close the mouth. The sound is blocked by the tongue, teeth, or lips. Today we will learn the sound that the letter Mm makes.

Q: Where can we find the story of Moses?
A: Class response… <u>*The Bible, Books in the Old Testament-Genesis, Exodus, Leviticus, Numbers,…*</u>

Today's story comes from the book of Exodus, the second book in the Old Testament. In Exodus 1:15-2:1-10, we read about the birth of Moses. We find out later that God had a very special job for Moses to do. Because God's people multiplied or increased very fast, the ruler of that time wanted the midwives (the women who delivered the babies) to kill every boy baby. The midwives feared God more than man. They refused to kill the boy babies of the people of God. But Pharaoh still wanted all boy Hebrew or Israelite babies to be thrown into the Nile river. When Moses' mother had given birth, she hid him in an ark in the Nile river to keep him from being killed. His sister watched him from afar. Pharaoh's daughter discovered him and raised Moses as her own son.

Moses' mother took care of him while Pharaoh's daughter raised him. This was part of God's plan to prepare him to save his people from slavery. Later in his life, Moses did exactly what God wanted him to do. We must be obedient to God, too. God loves us just as he loved Moses and the Israelite people.

Bible Verse: "Though he were a Son, yet learned he obedience by the things which he suffered" (Hebrews 5:08).

Teacher: Let me ask you some questions.
Q: Where is this story found in the Bible?
A: This story is found in the book of Exodus 1:15-2:1-10.
Q: What did Moses' mother do to save him from being destroyed?
A: Moses' mother hid him in an ark and placed him in the Nile river.
Q: Who found Moses?
A: Pharaoh's daughter found Moses and raised him as her own son.
Q: Do you think that God had a plan for Moses' life when he was a baby?
A: Answers will vary.
Q: Do you think that God has a plan for your life?
A: I believe that God has a plan for my life. Ask for examples.

Teacher: Ask students if they have any questions.
Activities: Refer to Activity Workbook, Lesson 13
Word Wall Words: Moses, milk,…

N
is for Noah

Lesson 14/Day 1-The Letter N

Text-Genesis 7:1-24

Teacher: Hello Boys and Girls,

I am so happy that you are in Bible Class (today or tonight). Thank you for being here. Today we are going to celebrate the letter Nn. The letter Nn is what is called a consonant.

Who remembers what a consonant is? Consonants are sounds that close the mouth. The sound is blocked by the tongue, teeth, or lips. Today we will learn the sound that the letter Nn makes.

Repeat it with me please, Nn, Nn, Noah. Nn, Nn, Noah.

Q: Where can we find the story of Noah?

A: Class response… *The Bible, Books in the Old Testament-Genesis, Exodus, Leviticus, Numbers,…*

Today's story comes from the book of Genesis, the first book in the Old Testament and the first book in the Bible. In Genesis 7:1-24, we read about Noah and the ark. God was sad that he had made man because man thought about doing evil all the time. God decided to destroy man.

He told Noah to build an ark. He wanted to save Noah and his family because Noah did good things instead of bad things. And this pleased God.

The ark was special. This ark was going to withstand a flood that would last forty (40) days. It was going to rain for forty (40) days. How high do you think the water rose in forty days? *Answers will vary.* It began to rain and rain and rain. God put Noah, his wife, his three sons and their wives and all the animals in the ark. God saved Noah and his family because Noah was obedient to God. We know that God takes care of those who are obedient to Him.

Bible Verse: "Much more then, being now justified by his blood, we shall be saved from wrath through him" (Romans 5:09).

Teacher: Let me ask you some questions.

Q: Where is this story found in the Bible?
A: *This story is found in the book of Genesis 7:1-24.*
Q: Why was God sad?
A: *God was sad he made man because man thought about doing bad things instead of doing good things.*
Q: What did God tell Noah to do?
A: *God told Noah to build an ark. And Noah was obedient to God.*
Q: How long did it rain?
A: *It rained for forty days.*
Q: How can you obey God?
A: *Answers will vary.*

Teacher: Ask students if they have any questions.

Activities: Refer to Activity Workbook, Lesson 14
Word Wall Words: Noah, night,…

O is for Obadiah

Lesson 15/Day 1-The Letter O

<u>Text-I Kings 18:1-4</u>

Teacher: Hello Boys and Girls,

I am so happy that you are in Bible Class (today or tonight). Thank you for being here. We are going to celebrate the letter Oo. The letter Oo is what is called a vowel.

Who remembers what a vowel is? Vowels can make a long or short sound. Today we will learn the sound that the letter Oo makes. For this lesson, this Oo sound makes a long sound. Repeat the sound with me please -Oo, Oo, Obadiah. Oo, Oo, Obadiah.

Q: Where can we find the story of Obadiah?
A: Class response… <u>*The Bible, Books in the Old Testament-Genesis, Exodus, Leviticus, Numbers,…*</u>

Today's story comes from the book of 1 Kings, the eleventh book in the Old Testament. In 1Kings 18:1-4, we read about King Ahab and the governor of his house, Obadiah. King Ahab ruled over Israel but he was an evil (bad) king. He married Jezebel and they worshipped Baal. Baal was considered to be a god of the storm and fertility.

When Jezebel killed some of the prophets of God, Obadiah took a hundred (100) prophets and hid them in two caves and took care of them. The Bible says in 1 Kings 18:04 that Obadiah fed them bread and water. Although, his boss, King Ahab did not believe in God, Obadiah believed in God. He did what was right in spite of how his boss acted. We should always do what God wants us to do no matter what others say.

Bible Verse: "If ye be willing and obedient, ye shall eat the good of the land" (Isaiah 1:09).

Teacher: Let me ask you some questions.
    Q: Where is this story found in the Bible?
    A: This story is found in the book of I Kings 18:01-04.
    Q: Who did Obadiah work for?
    A: Obadiah worked for King Ahab.
    Q: What did he do that King Ahab did not know about?
    A: Obadiah hid 100 prophets because King Ahab's wife, Jezebel had killed some prophets.
    Q: Should we always do what God wants us to do?
    A: Answers will vary.

Teacher: Ask students if they have any questions.
    Activities: Refer to Activity Workbook, Lesson 15
    Word Wall Words: Obadiah, oak,…

P
is for Paul

32

Lesson 16/Day 1-The Letter P

Text-Acts 9:1-19

Teacher: Hello Boys and Girls,

I am so happy that you are in Bible Class (today or tonight). Thank you for being here. We are going to celebrate the letter Pp. The letter Pp is what is called a consonant.

Who remembers what a consonant is? Consonants are sounds that close the mouth. The sound is blocked by the tongue, teeth, or lips. (Today or tonight) we will learn the sound that the letter Pp makes. Today, we will learn about Paul. Repeat it with me please-Pp, Pp, Paul, Pp, Pp, Paul.

Q: Where can we find the story of Saul/Paul?
A: Class response... *The Bible, Books in the New Testament Matthew, Mark, Luke, John Acts,...*

Today's story comes from the book of Acts, the fifth book in the New Testament. In Acts 9:01-19, Saul met Jesus on the Damascus Road. Saul was on his way to Damascus to hurt Christians, but Jesus stopped him on his way. Jesus asked Saul, "Saul why do you persecute me?" Saul had a repentant (changed) heart and decided to obey Jesus. Saul, was also called Paul (Acts 13:09).

In verse 18, Paul was baptized for the remission of his sins and became a Christian. I want to obey God so that I can become a Christian. God sent Paul to Ananias' home and Ananias taught him what to do to become a Christian.

Bible Verse: "Repent and be baptized, every one of you, in the name of Jesus Christ for the forgiveness of your sins. And you will receive the gift of the Holy Spirit" (Acts 2:38).

Teacher: Let me ask you some questions.
- Q: Where is this story found in the Bible?
- A: *This story is found in the book of Acts 9:01-23.*
- Q: What was Saul doing?
- A: *Paul was planning to do bad things to Christians.*
- Q: Who spoke to Saul on the Damascus road?
- A *Jesus spoke to Saul on the Damascus road.*
- Q: Where did Jesus send Saul to hear the gospel?
- A: *Jesus sent Saul to Ananias' house. Ananias taught Saul the gospel and then baptized him in the name of the Jesus Christ for the remission of his sins.*
- Q: After Saul met Jesus and became Christan he was known as _____
- A: *Paul.*

Teacher: Ask students if they have any questions.
Activities: Refer to Activity Workbook, Lesson 16
Word Wall Words: Paul, pan, put,...

Lesson 17/Day 1-The Letter Qu

Text-Esther

Teacher: Hello Boys and Girls,

I am so happy that you are in Bible Class (today or tonight). Thank you for being here. We are going to celebrate the letter Qq. The letter Qq is what is called a consonant.

Who remembers what a consonant is? A consonant is a sound that closes the mouth. The sound is blocked by the tongue, teeth, or lips. (Today or tonight) we will learn the sound that the letter Qu, qu makes. Repeat it with me please-Qu, qu, Qu, qu, Queen, Qu, qu, Qu, qu, Queen.

Q: Where can we find the story of Queen Esther?
A: Class response... *The Bible, in the book of Esther.*

Today's story comes from the book of Esther, the seventeenth book in the Old Testament. Esther was a beautiful queen. Esther was chosen to be the queen after Queen Vashti refused to obey King Ahasuerus' cruel rules.

There was an evil man who worked for King Ahasuerus named Haman. He wanted to destroy all the Jews in the kingdom. Haman's plan to destroy God's people actually ended up destroying him and his family. Because Esther was a Jew, God allowed Esther to talk to the king to save her people. God used Haman's evil plan to show how strong and mighty He really is. We can never be too smart or too strong for God. Haman and his family learned the hard way that disobeying God never works. God placed Esther in the position to save her people from destruction.

Bible Verse: "And who knoweth, whether thou art come to the kingdom for such a time as this" (Esther 4:14).

Teacher: Let me ask you some questions.
    Q: Where is this story found in the Bible?
    A: This story is found in the book of Esther.
    Q: Who is Esther?
    A: Esther is a Jew and becomes the queen after Vashti.
    Q: What did Esther do?
    A Esther saved the Jews from destruction.
    Q: Did Haman's plan work?
    A: Haman's plan did not work. We need to always obey God.

Teacher: Ask students if they have any questions.
    Activities: Refer to Activity Workbook, Lesson 17
    Word Wall Words: Queen, quail,...

R
is for Rebekah

Lesson 18/Day 1-The Letter R

Text-Genesis 27

Teacher: Hello Boys and Girls,

I am so happy that you are in Bible Class (today or tonight). Thank you for being here. We are going to celebrate the letter Rr. The letter Rr is what is called a consonant.

Who remembers what a consonant is? A consonant is a sound that closes the mouth. The sound is blocked by the tongue, teeth, or lips. Repeat it with me please-Rr, Rr, Rebekah, Rr, Rr, Rebekah.

Q: Where can we find the story of Rebekah?
A: Class response… *The Bible, In the book of Genesis.*

Today's story comes from the book of Genesis. Rebekah is married to Isaac, Abraham's son. They have twin sons. The oldest of their children is named Esau and their youngest son is named Jacob. God promised to bless Isaac because of the faithfulness of his father, Abraham. God kept his promise. Isaac and Rebekah became very, very rich. God always keeps his promises.

Rebekah loved Jacob and Isaac loved Esau. This became a problem in their family. Because Rebekah tricked Isaac, Jacob deceitfully received Esau's blessing. It was God's plan for Jacob to become great but it was not right for Rebekah to trick her husband Isaac. We should always wait for God instead of trying to do things our way. God will always work things out for our good.

Bible Verse: "And we know that all things work together for good to them that love God, to them who are the called according to his purpose" (Romans 8:28).

Teacher: Let me ask you some questions.
    Q: Where is this story found in the Bible?
    A: This story is found in the book of Genesis, chapter 27.
    Q: Who is Rebekah married to?
    A: Rebekah is married to Isaac, Abraham's son.
    Q: How many children did they have?
    A They had twin boys, Esau and Jacob.
    Q: What did Rebekah do?
    A: Rebekah tricked her husband Isaac into giving Jacob, Esau's blessing.

Teacher: Ask students if they have any questions.
    Activities: Refer to Activity book, Lesson 18
    Word Wall Words: Rebekah, run, race,…

S
is for Sapphira

Lesson 19/Day 1-The Letter S

<u>Text-Acts 4:32-37; 5:1-11</u>

Teacher: Hello Boys and Girls,

I am so happy that you are in Bible Class (today or tonight). Thank you for being here. We are going to celebrate the letter Ss. The letter Ss is what is called a consonant.

Who remembers what a consonant is? A consonant is a sound that closes the mouth. The sound is blocked by the tongue, teeth, or lips. Repeat the sound with me please -Ss, Ss, Sapphira. Ss, Ss, Sapphira.

Q: Where can we find the story of Sapphira?
A: Class response… *The Bible, In the book of Acts.*

Today's story comes from the book of Acts. There was a man and a woman who were members of the Church named Ananias and Sapphira. During this time in the Church, the members sold their possessions and gave to others. The Bible says in Acts 4:32 that, "they had all things in common." This means that Christians took care of each other and they shared everything that they had.

The people would bring their gifts to the apostles for distribution (sharing). Ananias lied and told the apostle Peter that this was all the money for the land that he and his wife collected. This was not the truth. Peter told him that this was not the truth and Ananias died at that moment. About three hours later, Sapphira walked in and told the apostle Peter that this was all the money collected from the sale of their land. She died as her husband had. The men collected her body and buried her alongside her husband.

Ananias and Sapphira lied to God. It is never good to lie to God because God already knows what you are thinking. They should have told the truth. Telling the truth is always better than lying. When we tell the truth, we can trust that God will help us to bear our consequences.

Bible Verse: "Nay, in all these things we are more than conquerors through him that loved us" (Romans 8:37).

Teacher: Let me ask you some questions.
Q: Where is this story found in the Bible?
A: This story is found in the book of Acts, chapters 4-5.
Q: Who are Ananias and Sapphira?
A: Ananias and Sapphira are members of the Church.
Q: What did they do?
A They sold their land but lied to God about the money they collected.
Q: What happened to them?
A: Because they lied to God, they both died.

Teacher: Ask students if they have any questions.
Activities: Refer to Activity book, Lesson 19
Word Wall Words: Sapphira, sat, sack,…

T
is for Thomas

Lesson 20/Day 1-The Letter T

<u>Text-John 20:24-29</u>

Teacher: Hello Boys and Girls,

I am so happy that you are in Bible Class (today or tonight). Thank you for being here. We are going to celebrate the letter Tt. The letter Tt is what is called a consonant.

Who remembers what a consonant is? A consonant is a sound that closes the mouth. The sound is blocked by the tongue, teeth, or lips. (Today or tonight) we will learn the sound that the letter Tt makes. Repeat the sound with me please -Tt, Tt, Thomas. Tt, Tt, Thomas.

Q: Where can we find the story of Thomas?
A: Class response… *The Bible, In the book of John.*

Today's story comes from the book of John. The book of John is in the New Testament. Thomas was one of the disciples chosen to share the good news about Jesus to the Jews. After Jesus had been crucified, he was resurrected on the first day of the week which is Sunday. Not all of the disciples were there when it was discovered that Jesus was alive. Thomas was not there. But when the other disciples shared the good news of Jesus' resurrection, Thomas said, "Except I shall see in his hands the print of the nails, and put my finger into the print of the nails, and thrust my hand into his side, I will not believe," vs. 25.

When Jesus appeared again to his disciples, Thomas was there. He had a chance to touch Jesus and then he believed that he had risen from the dead. Faith is believing God even when we cannot see what he is doing or what is happening.

Bible Verse: "Blessed are they that have not seen, and yet have believed" (John 20:29).

Teacher: Let me ask you some questions.
  Q: Where is this story found in the Bible?
  A: This story is found in the book of John, Chapter 20.
  Q: Who was Thomas?
  A: Thomas was a disciple of Jesus Christ.
  Q: What happened after Jesus had been resurrected?
  A Thomas because he was not there did not believe the news of Jesus' resurrection.
  Q: What did Thomas say?
  A: Thomas said that he would have to feel the imprint of the nails in his hand and feel the piercing in his side before he would believe that Jesus had been resurrected.
  Q: Did Thomas finally believe?
  A: After Jesus reappeared, he allowed Thomas to touch him so that he would believe.

Teacher: Ask students if they have any questions.
  Activities: Refer to Activity book, Lesson 20
  Word Wall Words: Thomas, them, thick,…

U
is for Uriah

Lesson 21/Day 1-The Letter U

<u>Text-2 Samuel 11:1-27</u>

Teacher: Hello Boys and Girls,

I am so happy that you are in Bible Class today or tonight. Thank you for being here. We are going to celebrate the letter Uu. The letter Uu is what is called a vowel.

Who remembers what a vowel is? Vowels can also make a long or short sound.

(Today or tonight) we will learn the sound that the letter Uu makes in this lesson is a long sound. Repeat the sound with me please -Uu Uu, Uriah. Uu, Uu, Uriah.

Q: Where can we find the story of Uriah?
A: Class response… *<u>The Bible, In the book of 2 Samuel.</u>*

Today's story comes from the book of 2 Samuel 11:01-27. The book of 2 Samuel is in the Old Testament. Uriah was a soldier in King David's army. He was a good soldier, too. He cared so much about King David and his army. He believed in David's God, as well. His name meant, "God is my light". Uriah was married to a woman named Bathsheba. He was so devoted to King David that he left his wife and lived and fought with the other soldiers.

Uriah's wife, Bathsheba was very pretty. King David decided that he would take her like she was his wife. Uriah was so committed to fighting in the battle with the king's soldiers that he did not know what King David had done. As a result of his loyalty to King David, he died serving King David.

Bible Verse: "Thou shalt love the Lord thy God with all thy soul, and with all thy strength, and with all thy mind; and thy neighbor as thyself" (Luke 10:27).

Teacher: Let me ask you some questions.
   Q: Where is this story found in the Bible?
   A: This story is found in the book of 2 Samuel, chapter 11.
   Q: Who was Uriah?
   A: Uriah was a soldier in King David's army.
   Q: What did Uriah do during the time of war?
   A Uriah fought with the other soldiers. He was devoted to King David and his army.
   Q: What does Uriah mean?
   A: Uriah means, "God is my light".
   Q: What can we learn about the devotion of Uriah?
   A: We can learn that God wants us to be devoted wholly to Him.

Teacher: Ask students if they have any questions.
   Activities: Refer to Activity Workbook, Lesson 21
   Word Wall Words: Uriah, unicorn,…

V is for Vashti

Lesson 22/Day 1-The Letter V

Text-Esther 1:10-12;19

Teacher: Hello Boys and Girls,
    I am so happy that you are in Bible Class (today or tonight). Thank you for being here. We are going to celebrate the letter Vv. The letter Vv is what is called a consonant.
    Who remembers what a consonant is? A consonant is a sound that closes the mouth. The sound is blocked by the tongue, teeth, or lips. (Today or tonight) we will learn the sound that the letter Vv makes. Vv, Vv, Vashti. Vv, Vv, Vashti.
    Q: Where can we find the story of Queen Vashti?
    A: Class response... *The Bible, In the book of Esther.*

Today's story comes from the book of Esther 1:10-12;19. The book of Esther is in the Old Testament. Queen Vashti took a very bold stand against her husband King Xerxes. King Xerxes decided to give a week long banquet for all his nobles and officials. He sent for the queen on the seventh (7th) day of his banquet. He wanted her to wear her royal crown and prance around so that everyone could see how beautiful she was.

The Bible states that Queen Vashti was a very beautiful woman. In other words, he wanted to disgrace her in front of his drunk friends. Have you ever been in a situation where a friend embarrasses you to the point where you want to run and hide? This is the way I picture Queen Vashti. Queen Vashti said, emphatically **NO**. This was very bold on her part because you don't ever say **NO** to the king. But she refused to be disgraced in front of the drunk king and his intoxicated friends. The significance of this story is two-fold in that Queen Vashti refused to be embarrassed by the king and by her refusal she opened the door for Esther to become Queen and save her people, the Jews, from destruction.

Bible Verse: "If God be for us, who can be against us" (Romans 8:31).

Teacher: Let me ask you some questions.
    Q: Where is this story found in the Bible?
    A: *This story is found in the book of Esther, chapter 1.*
    Q: Who was Vashti?
    A: *Vashti was the wife of King Xerxes.*
    Q: What did Queen Vashti do?
    A *She refused to be disgraced by the king at his banquet for his nobles and officials.*
    Q: What can we learn from Queen Vashti?
    A: *Answers will vary. We can learn that we can stand up to bullies with God on our side.*

Teacher: Ask students if they have any questions.
    Activities: Refer to Activity Workbook, Lesson 22
    Word Wall Words: Vashti, van, vowel,...

W
is for Woman at the well

Lesson 23/Day 1-The Letter W

Text-John 4:1-42

Teacher: Hello Boys and Girls,

I am so happy that you are in Bible Class (today or tonight). Thank you for being here. We are going to celebrate the letter Ww. The letter Ww is what is called a consonant.

Who remembers what a consonant is? A consonant is a sound that closes the mouth. The sound is blocked by the tongue, teeth, or lips. (Today or tonight) we will learn the sound that the letter Ww makes. Ww, Ww, Ww, Woman at the Well, Ww, Ww, Ww, Woman at the Well.

Q: Where can we find the story of the Samaritan Woman?
A: Class response… *The Bible, In the book of John.*

Today's story comes from the book of John, chapter 4:01-42. The book of John is the fourth book in the New Testament. This story is the revelation of God's love to those who are seen as less than other people, even when it comes to being accepted by God. Jews and Samaritans did not hang out together. This is because of some bad history that occurred when Jews were slaves in Babylonia. It sort of reminds me of how blacks were enslaved by whites and whites and blacks did not get along with each other.

Anyway, Jesus was on his way back to Galilee and he had to pass through a town in Samaria named Sychar. He stopped at Jacob's well because he was tired. Later a Samaritan woman came to draw water and Jesus asked her for a drink. Jesus ended up telling this woman everything that she had ever done and she ran into town and shared what Jesus said to her.

Jesus also told the Samaritan woman that the water that he could give her would be living water and that she would never thirst again. Because of his words, many Samaritans became believers (vs. 39).

Jesus told the Samaritan woman that "God is a Spirit, and all who worship him must worship him in Spirit and in truth" (vs.24) Jesus showed the Samaritan woman that it didn't matter what she looked like or what her background was, it was only important that she Believe. It is important, boys and girls, that you believe and obey what Jesus tells you to do.

Bible Verse: "God is spirit, and his worshipers must worship in Spirit and in truth" (John 4:24).

Teacher: Let me ask you some questions.
Q: Where is this story found in the Bible?
A: *This story is found in the book of John, chapter 4:01-42.*
Q: Who was the Woman at the Well?
A: *The woman at the well was actually a Samaritan woman who came to Jacob's well to draw water.*
Q: What was Jesus doing at the well?
A *Jesus was on his way to Galilee and had to pass through Sychar (in Samaria).*
Q: Why was this an unusual situation?
A: *Because Jews and Samaritans did not mix or even talk with each other.*
Q: What can we learn from the way Jesus and the Woman at the Well talked with each other?
A: *We can learn that God wants everyone to be saved. It doesn't matter what you look like or how you speak. Answers will vary.*

Teacher: Ask students if they have any questions.
Refer to Activity Workbook, Lesson 23
Word Wall Words: Woman at the Well, wagon, well,…

X is for Xerxes

Lesson 24/Day 1-The Letter X

Text-Esther 1-2:

Teacher: Hello Boys and Girls,

I am so happy that you are in Bible Class (today or tonight). Thank you for being here. We are going to celebrate the letter Xx. The letter Xx is what is called a consonant.

Who remembers what a consonant is? A consonant is a sound that closes the mouth. The sound is blocked by the tongue, teeth, or lips. (Today or tonight) we will learn the sound that the letter Xx makes. Xx, Xx, Xerxes. Xx, Xx, Xerxes.

Q: Where can we find the story of King Xerxes?
A: Class response... *The Bible, In the book of Esther.*

Today's story comes from the book of Esther, chapters 1-2. The book of Esther is in the Old Testament. King Xerxes was a very powerful king. He ruled over 127 provinces or areas from India to Cush. King Xerxes decided to give a party for all the people who worked for him. The party lasted for 180 days and then he decided to give a banquet for seven days. He displayed all his wealth and his riches to his friends. Wow imagine that. Have you ever had a party for 180 days or six months? He also wanted to display his beautiful queen, Vashti.

When Queen Vashti refused to be put on display in front of the king and his friends, he ultimately chooses Esther to be the next queen. God used Xerxes and King Xerxes chose Esther to be queen to save her people, the Jews, from being destroyed.

Bible Verse: "Let thy mercy, O Lord, be upon us, according as we hope in thee" (Psalm 33:22).

Teacher: Let me ask you some questions.
Q: Where is this story found in the Bible?
A: This story is found in the book of Esther, chapters 1-2.
Q: Who was Xerxes?
A: Xerxes was a king.
Q: What did King Xerxes do?
A He gave a party for 180 days followed by a banquet for seven more days to show off all his wealth and riches. He wanted to embarrass his wife, Queen Vashti.
Q: What can we learn from King Xerxes?
A: Answers will vary. We can learn that being rich does not make you more powerful than God. King Xerxes ended up being a part of God's plan to save God's people, the Jews.

Teacher: Ask students if they have any questions.
Activities: Refer to Activity Workbook, Lesson 24
Word Wall Words: Xerxes, x-ray, Xerox,...

Y
is for Yahweh

Lesson 25/Day 1-The Letter Y

<u>Text-Genesis 1:1;26; John 1:1-5; Revelation 22:17-21</u>

Teacher: Hello Boys and Girls,

I am so happy that you are in Bible Class (today or tonight). Thank you for being here. We are going to celebrate the letter Yy. The letter Yy is what is called a consonant.

Who remembers what a consonant is? A consonant is a sound that closes the mouth. The sound is blocked by the tongue, teeth, or lips. Sometimes on special occasions the letter Yy can also sound like a vowel as in the word why. In the word why, the Yy makes a long Ii sound. We have learned that in our language we basically have five (5) vowels-A, E, I, O, U and sometimes Y only on special occasions. Who remembers what a vowel is? A vowel is a sound that can make a long or short sound. We will learn the sound that the letter Yy makes. Yy, Yy, Yahweh. Yy, Yy, Yahweh.

In the beginning God created the heavens and the earth. In Genesis chapter 1, the Bible tells about all the beautiful things that God created. On the sixth day, God, Jesus, and the Holy Spirit decided to make man in his own image. Because scripture says in Genesis 1:26, "Let us make mankind in our image in our likeness to rule over all creatures". God, Jesus, and the Holy Spirit were there together at the beginning.

In the New Testament, John begins his book with the testimony that Jesus was with God in the beginning of time and that when it was His time to be revealed in the form of a human being, God sent his only begotten Son to save the world from their sins (John 3:16).

At the end of time, God, Jesus, and the Holy Spirit will come back to get those who have believed and obeyed what God has told them to do. God tells us what he wants us to do in the Bible.

Yahweh means Jehovah. Jehovah is the name that can only be given to God. Our God is omnipotent, omniscient, and omnipresent which means that Jehovah God is all-powerful, all-knowing, and everywhere. Yahweh is Everything!

Bible Verse: "For in Him we live, and move, and have our very being" (Acts 17:28).

Teacher: Let me ask you some questions.
- Q: Where can we find the story of Yahweh?
- A: Class response... *<u>The Bible, the whole book tells of God's plan to save the world.</u>*
- Q: Where is <u>this</u> story found in the Bible?
- *A: This story is found in the books of Genesis, John, and Revelation.*
- Q: What does Yahweh mean?
- *A: Yahweh is another name for Jehovah.*
- Q: Is Yahweh stronger than Superman or Batman?
- *A Yahweh is stronger than Superman, Batman or anyone or anything in the whole universe.*
- Q: What do we know about Jehovah or Yahweh?
- *A: We know that Jehovah or Yahweh is all-powerful, all-knowing, and everywhere at the same time.*

Teacher: Ask students if they have any questions.
Activities: Refer to Activity Workbook, Lesson 25
Word Wall Words: Yahweh, yoyo, yard,...

Lesson 26/Day 1-The Letter Z

<u>Text-Luke 19:1-10</u>

Teacher: Hello Boys and Girls,

I am so happy that you are in Bible Class (today or tonight). Thank you for being here. We are going to celebrate the letter Zz. The letter Zz is what is called a consonant.

Who remembers what a consonant is? A consonant is a sound that closes the mouth. The sound is blocked by the tongue, teeth, or lips. (Today or tonight) we will learn the sound that the letter Zz makes. Zz, Zz, Zacchaeus. Zz, Zz, Zacchaeus.

Q: Where can we find the story of Zacchaeus?
A: Class response… <u>The Bible, In the book of Luke.</u>

Today's story comes from the book of Luke 19:01-10. The book of Luke is in the New Testament. Luke is the third (3rd) book in the New Testament. Zacchaeus had two things against him-first he was a tax collector and the second was that he was very, very short. Being a tax collector meant that he collected money (taxes) that were owed to the Roman government. As you might imagine, Zacchaeus was not well liked. People didn't like the idea of having to give their money to Zacchaeus to pay their taxes. The Bible even inferred that sometimes Zacchaeus wasn't very honest with people and took more money than he needed to.

Well, one day when Jesus was passing through Jericho, Zacchaeus wanted to see him. Because he was so short, he had to climb up a sycamore tree to see Jesus. Jesus is so smart that when he got to the tree, he looked up and saw Zacchaeus. Jesus told Zacchaeus that he would stay at his house that night. Because of Jesus, Zacchaeus decided to give half of his possessions to the poor and to give four (4) times back the money he may have cheated anyone out of. Isn't it amazing to see what God can do in all our lives?

Bible Verse: "People look at the outward appearance, but the Lord looks at the heart" (1Samuel 16:07b).

Teacher: Let me ask you some questions.
Q: Where is this story found in the Bible?
A: This story is found in the book of Luke, chapter 19:01-10.
Q: Who was Zacchaeus?
A: Zacchaeus was a tax collector.
Q: What did Zacchaeus do when Jesus passed through Jericho?
A He wanted to see Jesus so he climbed up a sycamore tree to see Jesus.
Q: What can we learn from Zacchaeus?
A: Answers will vary. We can learn from Zacchaeus that if we want to know about Jesus, Jesus will make it possible.

Teacher: Ask students if they have any questions.
Activities: Refer to Activity Workbook, Lesson 26
Word Wall Words: Zacchaeus, zebra, zoom, zag,…

Bible Phonics ABC Song

Oh!
"A" goes ahahah
"B" goes buhbuh,
"C" goes cuh cuh and
"D" goes duh
"E" goes eh eh eh
"F" goes [F] [F]
"G" goes guh guh guh and
"H" goes [H]
"I" goes ih ih ih
"J" goes juh juh
"K" goes kuh kuh kuh
"L" goes [L]
"M" goes muh muh muh
"N" goes nuh nuh
"O" goes ah ah ah and
"P" goes puh
"Q" goes kuh kuh kuh
"R" goes ruh ruh
"S" goes suh suh suh and
"T" goes tuh
"U" goes uh uh uh
"V" goes vuh vuh
"W" goes wuh wuh wuh and
"X" goes [ks]
"Y" goes yuh yuh yuh
"Z" goes zuh zuh

Great job that's all the letters shout Hurray! Hurray!

WORKBOOK

Aa Aa Aa Aa Aa

Adam Adam Adam

God created Adam

on the sixth day.

FILL IN THE BLANKS
A is for Adam

1. _____ was the first man that God created.

2. God created Adam on the _____ day.

3. God made Adam out of the _____ of the ground.

4. After God created a _____ and a _____, he was _____ with his work.

5. On the _____ day, God rested

Draw a picture of the Garden of Eden.

word search

```
C Z U G H L M A N
R E S T E D O T O
E W D P F C O A Q
A N S C H Z N M D
T B V M T N L R M
I Q K E R J I A A
O Y W M A E R O D
N E V A E H X B A
```

ADAM   HEAVEN   RESTED
MOON   EARTH   CREATION
              MAN

Bb Bb Bb Bb Bb

Baal Baal Baal

Baal was not the

true God.

FILL IN THE BLANKS
B is for Baal

1. The story of Baal is found in 1 Kings _____.

2. Elijah challenged the _____ of Baal.

3. Elijah told King _____ that the living God was _____ than their god, Baal.

4. The prophets of Baal called on their _____ from morning until evening, but their _____ did not answer them.

5. There were 450 _____ of Baal against _____ on Mount Carmel.

Describe Elijah. (WORD OR PICTURE)

word search

B	D	E	L	I	J	A	H	Q
E	H	T	U	S	N	F	Z	S
B	G	W	I	K	K	I	N	G
D	Z	Q	S	J	I	R	U	O
A	C	M	R	W	N	E	X	R
H	P	O	A	R	M	K	L	J
A	H	V	E	X	G	F	C	T
B	A	A	L	P	G	O	D	V

BAAL
ELIJAH

AHAB
GOD
FIRE

ISRAEL
KING

Cc Cc Cc Cc Cc

Cain Cain Cain

Cain killed his

brother Abel.

FILL IN THE BLANKS
C is for Cain

1. Abel made an _____ offering and Cain did not.

2. Cain got so _____ that he killed his brother.

3. When Cain _____ his brother, it made God sad.

4. God sent _____ away for what he did.

5. Cain sinned against God and against his _____.

Draw a picture of Cain's offering.

word search

```
G O F F E R I N G
F H B N O A Z O Y
M E R M N Q L J S
P L O A N G R Y I
N B T V D C S D N
I W H R Q U B X N
A B E L S A K W E
C Z R K I L L E D
```

CAIN OFFERING BROTHER
ABEL ANGRY   SINNED
      KILLED

D is for Devil

Dd Dd Dd Dd Dd

Devil Devil Devil

The devil deceived

Eve and Adam.

FILL IN THE BLANKS
D is for Devil

1. They could eat of any tree in the _____ ____ _____ except the tree that was in the middle of the garden.

2. The _____ talked them into eating from the tree that God told them not to.

3. God told them that if they ate from that _____, they would _____.

4. Because of their _____, Adam and _____ were disciplined by God.

5. Although God had to teach _____ and _____ a lesson, he still loved them.

AAMD _____

VEDLI _____

IIEEEODSNBDC _____

RDNGAE _____

NWMAO _____

VELDO _____

UNSCRAMBLE

word search

```
D E V I L B V A M
Q V N Y S T U R D
H E W O M A N C I
O F D B J V Q Z E
E B G E D N A M U
K L H Y P E O T X
X W E Y F D C I W
Z O P E S E L U R
```

DEVIL RULES EVE
OBEY   EDEN   DIE
       WOMAN

Ee Ee Ee Ee Ee

Enoch Enoch Enoch

Enoch walked with

God and God took

him.

TRUE OR FALSE
E is for Enoch

_____ 1. The story of Enoch comes from the book of Exodus, the first book in the Bible.

_____ 2. In our lesson text, the Bible tells us that Enoch walked with God.

_____ 3. Enoch did not die, for God took him.

_____ 4. Enoch's father, Methuselah, died at the age of 962.

_____ 5. Enoch's son, Jared, died at the age of 969.

_____ 6. God took Enoch when he was 365 years old.

Write a poem about Enoch.

word search

```
S E D H W U K M E
Z L E B A S C P N
O B H R L Q M E O
T I V V K P A L C
C B N I E K J F H
J A R E D I N Y W
F G U O W Z O G T
G E N E S I S A N
```

ENOCH JARED BIBLE
WALKED SON AGE
  GENESIS

F
is for Festus

Ff Ff Ff Ff Ff Ff

Festus Festus

Festus was a

government

official.

FILL IN THE BLANKS
F is for Festus

1. Festus was a member of the _____.

2. It was God working through Festus that allowed _____ to speak about _____ to him.

3. God did not allow the _____ leaders to take Paul to _____ where they were planning to kill him.

4. God can and will _____ take care of you (I _____ 5: 07).

5. We should always want to obey _____ because He loves us so much.

WIESJH _____

TFSSEU _____

LDREEAS _____

OGD _____

TEERP _____

CATS _____

UNSCRAMBLE

word search

```
F E S T U S O O L
A G H A N M J R A
C P Z X V W E Y W
G A U X W W W Z A
A U T H O R I T Y
C L P V L T S Y U
T B E E L F H M P
S I O J A K L Q C
```

FESTUS
ACTS
PAUL
LAW
AUTHORITY
ALLOW
JEWISH

G
is for Goliath

Gg Gg Gg Gg Gg

Goliath Goliath

Goliath was a

giant.

TRUE OR FALSE
G is for Goliath

_____ 1. Goliath was a giant who stood nine feet tall.

_____ 2. David was the youngest of Jesse's sons.

_____ 3. Before he fought Goliath, David fought a lion and a bear and with God's help killed them both.

_____ 4. David was given permission to fight Goliath by King Ahab.

_____ 5. David killed Goliath with a sword and shield.

Draw a sling and a smooth stone.

word search

```
G I A T T N A I G
B J E S S E R S O
D S U L L R P K L
I A V I H S D J I
V K Z N G Y M R A
A N M G D W E C T
D Q F J A T H F H
A R M O R B U Y X
```

GOLIATH SLING JESSE
ARMY DAVID GIANT
  ARMOR

H
is for Hagar

Hh Hh Hh Hh Hh

Hagar Hagar

Hagar was Sarai's

handmaiden.

TRUE OR FALSE
H is for Hagar

_____ 1. Sarai was the handmaid of Hagar.

_____ 2. Sarai told her husband to have a child with Hagar.

_____ 3. God promised that Hagar's son would be a mighty nation.

_____ 4. Abram was ninety-six years old when his son with Hagar named Ishmael was born.

_____ 5. God sees you. His eyes see everything that we do.

Name some things a handmaiden might do.

word search

```
I L E A M H S I S
A M Y L I M A F T
W I F E S D R X I
E N Q U L C A O F
H A N D M A I D U
B K P A Z V A B W
G R H U S B A N D
H A G A R H J W Y
```

HAGAR   FAMILY   WIFE
SARAI   HUSBAND   ISHMAEL
            HANDMAID

Ii Ii Ii Ii Ii Ii Ii

Isaac Isaac Isaac

Isaac was the son

of Abraham.

TRUE OR FALSE
I is for Isaac

_____ 1. In Genesis 21, Sarah had not had any children.

_____ 2. When Sarah had a son, Abraham named him Isaac.

_____ 3. Abraham was a hundred years old when Isaac was born.

_____ 4. God tested Abraham by telling Abraham to sacrifice his only Son as a burnt offering. Abraham refused God.

_____ 5. Before he was to sacrifice Isaac on the altar, God provided a ram and Abraham did not have to offer his only son as a burnt offering to God.

Define in your own words:

Sacrifice-

Burnt Offering-

Ram in the Bush-

word search

S	A	C	R	I	F	I	C	E
T	N	R	U	B	D	O	Q	X
A	Z	P	M	T	S	U	R	T
C	Q	L	O	H	F	K	D	G
A	H	P	R	O	M	I	S	E
A	E	U	X	S	T	N	T	M
S	A	B	R	A	H	A	M	A
I	C	K	N	M	W	V	U	R

ISAAC ABRAHAM TRUST
PROMISE BURNT RAM
  SACRIFICE

J is for Jacob

Jj Jj Jj Jj Jj Jj

Jacob Jacob

Jacob tricked

Esau out of his

birthright

FILL IN THE BLANKS
J is for Jacob

1. Jacob's father's name was _____.

2. Isaac is the son of _____ and Sarah.

3. Isaac grows up and marries a woman named _____

4. Isaac and Rebekah have twin sons, named _____ and _____.

5. Esau's skin was _____, whereas, Jacob's skin was _____ (Gen. 27:11).

List ways in which twins are the same. Compare	List ways in which twins are different. Contrast

word search

```
U A S E E X S V O
D G N O L D E S T
S O I N H K L P W
K P W V C B S X R
I C T I S O U P U
N B M K F C E T N
A I Y R I A H H R
S A O Q B J D A M
```

JACOB   TWINS   OLDEST
ESAU   SKIN   SOUP
         HAIRY

is for Kenites

Kk Kk Kk Kk Kk

Kenites Kenites

The Kenite people

worked with

bronze and iron.

TRUE OR FALSE
K is for Kenite

_____ 1. Abraham's father-in-law, Jethro, was a Kenite.

_____ 2. Jethro was a shepherd and priest who lived in the land of Midian.

_____ 3. The Kenites journeyed with the Israelites to the land of Canaan.

_____ 4. King Ahab did not want to destroy the Kenites with the Amalekites who lived in the city of Amalek.

_____ 5. Historically, the Kenites were nomadic, meaning that they traveled around.

_____ 6. The Kenites invented working with bronze and iron, playing musical instruments, and creating art.

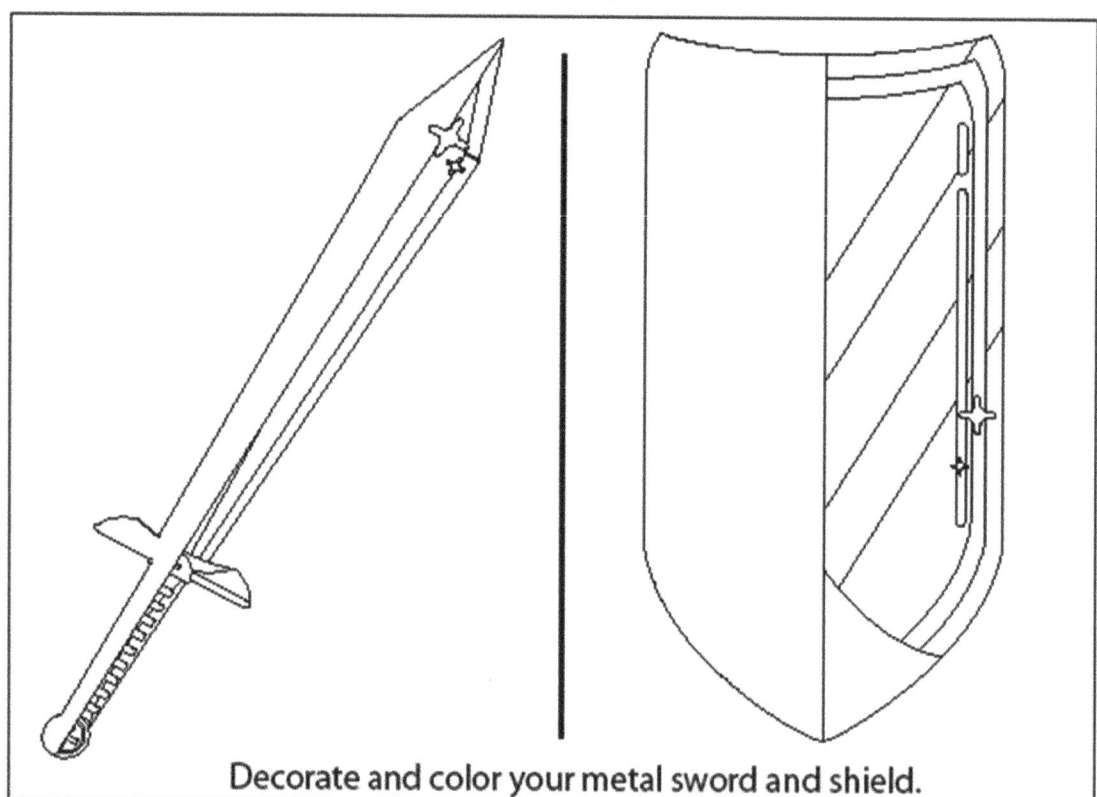

Decorate and color your metal sword and shield.

word search

```
N O M A D I C T P
K U S E T I N E K
E G Y P T O A R E
Z W Z R V R C D L
N M B I F H N S A
O Z N E X T P U M
R X R S O E W V A
B E D T C J G Q L
```

KENITES PRIEST NOMADIC
JETHRO   EGYPT   BRONZE
         AMALEK

Lazarus   Lazarus

Lazarus became

very sick and died.

FILL IN THE BLANKS
L is for Lazarus

1. The story of Lazarus comes from the book of _____ in the New Testament.

2. Lazarus had two sisters, _____ and _____.

3. Mary and Martha's brother got real _____ and _____.

4. _____ died and was buried four days before Jesus got back to Bethany where he lived.

5. _____ brought Lazarus back to life.

6. _____ is able to do whatever we believe Him to do.

Turn the page sideways and create a bookmark from today's memory verse.

word search

S	U	R	A	Z	A	L	F	M
N	B	G	H	J	D	I	G	A
H	E	D	O	E	P	M	R	R
O	F	E	I	R	Q	M	E	T
J	A	R	W	U	W	A	T	H
Y	U	O	X	S	X	R	S	A
B	E	T	H	A	N	Y	I	Z
S	B	D	V	Y	Q	P	S	L

LAZARUS   MARY   SISTER
JOHN   MARTHA   BURIED
          BETHANY

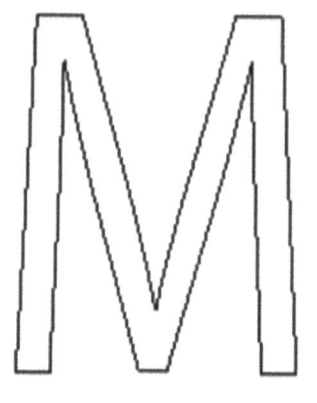

is for Moses

Mm Mm Mm Mm

Moses Moses

Moses was hidden

in the river by his

mother.

TRUE OR FALSE
M is for Moses

_____ 1. When Moses' mother had him, she hid him in an ark in the river to keep him from being killed.

_____ 2. Pharaoh's daughter found Moses in the river and raised Moses as her own son.

_____ 3. Moses' mother left Moses and went to another country while Pharaoh's daughter raised him.

_____ 4. God's plan was to prepare Moses to further enslave his people.

_____ 5. Moses did exactly what God wanted him to do.

_____ 6. God loves us just as he loved Moses and the Israelite people.

Create a picture of the palace where Moses grew up.

word search

```
P H A R A O H R M
S U D O X E Y E V
E S G A R R Z T U
A F H E E T G H B
B D K V H N F G M
C E A A T J C U N
D L W S O H V A K
S E S O M X S D U
```

MOSES   PHARAOH   SAVE
MOTHER   EXODUS   SLAVERY
                DAUGHTER

N
is for Noah

Nn Nn Nn Nn Nn

Noah Noah Noah

God told Noah to

build an ark.

TRUE OR FALSE
N is for Noah

_____ 1. In Exodus 7:3-24, we read about Noah and the ark.

_____ 2. God was sad that he made man and decided to destroy man. He told Moses to build an ark.

_____ 3. It was going to rain for eighty days.

_____ 4. God put Noah, his wife, his three sons and their wives and all the animals in the ark.

_____ 5. God saved Noah and his family because Noah was obedient to God.

_____ 6. God takes cares of those who are obedient to Him.

COMPARE	CONTRAST
Draw a picture of the Ark Noah was in.	Now draw a picture of the Ark Moses was in.

word search

A	R	K	F	I	O	W	T	A
L	A	M	Q	P	Q	V	N	T
B	G	I	D	R	A	I	N	F
D	E	F	O	M	M	K	H	D
L	J	N	O	A	H	L	O	S
I	W	K	L	U	E	J	C	R
U	B	S	F	O	R	T	Y	P
B	A	N	U	V	D	N	C	A

NOAH   BUILD   ANIMALS
ARK   FLOOD   RAIN
       FORTY

is for Obadiah

Oo Oo Oo Oo Oo

Obadiah Obadiah

Obadiah worked

for King Ahab.

FILL IN THE BLANKS
O is for Obadiah

1. Obadiah worked for King _____, but Obadiah believed in God.

2. King Ahab ruled over Israel but he was an _____ king.

3. King Ahab married _____ and they worshipped _____.

4. When _____ killed some of the prophets of the Lord, Obadiah took a hundred (100) prophets and hid them in two _____ and took care of them.

5. The Bible says in 1 Kings 18: 4 that Obadiah fed them _____ and _____.

CROSSWORD

ACROSS
1. Worked for King Ahab
2. Ahab's wife
3. Jezebel killed some of the ? of the Lord
4. Obadiah hid some of the prophets and fed them ? and water

DOWN
1. Jezebel and her husband ? Baal
2. This King did not believe in Obadiah's God.
3. Ahab was an _ _ _ _ King
4. Baal was considered to be a god of _ _ _ _ _ and fertility.

word search

I	O	B	Q	M	N	P	H	L
F	E	R	T	I	L	I	T	Y
U	D	E	R	W	Z	H	K	S
A	S	A	V	Q	K	S	G	T
E	M	D	L	I	P	R	W	O
H	A	I	D	A	B	O	T	R
B	V	R	C	D	F	W	A	M
E	V	E	I	L	E	B	I	B

OBADIAH   FERTILITY   STORM
EVIL   BREAD   BELIEVE
          WORSHIP

P is for Paul

Pp Pp Pp Pp Pp Pp

Paul Paul Paul Paul

Paul repented and

became a Christian

TRUE OR FALSE
P is for Paul

_____1. Saul met Jesus on the Damascus Road.

_____2. Saul was on his way to Damascus to baptize Christians.

_____3. Jesus asked Saul, "Saul why do you persecute me?"

_____4. Paul had a repentant (changed) heart and decided to obey Jesus.

_____5. God sent Paul to Timothy's home and Timothy taught him what to do to become a Christian.

_____6. Paul was baptized for the remission of his sins and became a Christian.

Tell the story of the conversion of Saul to Paul in story book form.

Once upon a time...

word search

```
D A M A S C U S R
A B A P T I Z E D
E T U C E S R E P
G C D M O N S Q A
N E Q F D E B C U
A N A N I A S T L
H G B A C E W V P
C H R I S T I A N
```

PAUL CHRISTIAN BAPTIZED
DAMASCUS PERSECUTE CHANGE
ANANIAS

is for Queen

Qq Qq Qq Qq Qq

Queen Queen

Queen Esther saved

her people from

destruction.

FILL IN THE BLANKS
Q is for Queen

1. Esther was a beautiful _____.

2. Esther was chosen to be the queen after Queen _____ refused to obey King Ahasuerus' cruel rules.

3. There was an evil man who worked for the King Ahasuerus named _____.

4. He wanted to destroy all the _____ in the kingdom.

5. Haman's plan to destroy God's people ended up destroying _____ and his _____.

6. God placed _____ in the position to _____ her people from destruction.

Name ten (10) qualities a Queen should have.

word search

```
L U F I T U A E B
I X R T A P D O Q
N D E H Q U E E N
A W H S F G S B H
M V T A B C U P U
A E S V C E F V N
H R E W G D E Z O
A H A S U E R U S
```

QUEEN VASHTI HAMAN
BEAUTIFUL ESTHER REFUSED
AHASUERUS

is for Rebekah

Rr Rr Rr Rr Rr Rr

Rebekah Rebekah

Rebekah was the

mother of Jacob

and Esau.

TRUE OR FALSE
R is for Rebekah

_____ 1. Rebekah was married to Isaac, Abraham's son.

_____ 2. They had twin sons. The oldest of their children was named Jacob and their youngest son was named Esau.

_____ 3. Isaac and Rebekah became poor because Abraham did not do what God asked him to do.

_____ 4. God always keeps his promises. But there were problems in the family.

_____ 5. Rebekah loved Jacob and Isaac loved Esau.

_____ 6. Because Rebekah tricked Isaac, Jacob and Esau's lost their blessings.

UESA   _____

CBOJA   _____

MAHARBA   _____

KAEREHB   _____

AACSI   _____

DGO   _____

UNSCRAMBLE THESE NAMES

word search

```
D Z E E H A U C H
P C A A S I A W A
F O L H M Y S Z K
P R O M I S E G E
O D V G T Q G N B
C N E D A X O K E
T R I C K E D U R
X B Q B Y S T I K
```

REBEKAH GOD   LOVE
TRICKED ESAU PROMISE
         ISAAC

S is for Sapphira

Ss Ss Ss Ss Ss Ss

Sapphira Sapphira

Sapphira died

because she lied

to God.

TRUE OR FALSE
S is for Sapphira

_____ 1. There was a man and a woman who were members of the Church of Christ named Ananias and Sapphira.

_____ 2. Ananias and Sapphira lied about the money he and his wife collected for their land.

_____ 3. Ananias and Sapphira lied to God and they died because of it.

_____ 4. It is never good to lie to God because God already knows what you are thinking.

_____ 5. Telling the truth is always better than lying.

CROSSWORD

ACROSS
1. Ananias' wife
2. People brought these to the altar to share with others
3. Another word for not telling the truth
4. It is always good to tell God the ?

DOWN
1. Ananias and his wife had to ___ for not being honest
2. Peter was one
3. Sapphira's husband
4. The body was the ? of Christ

word search

A	P	O	S	T	L	E	S	H
K	E	L	I	E	D	P	R	A
H	T	U	R	T	P	T	X	H
O	A	I	F	S	F	Y	C	Z
W	M	T	K	I	J	R	R	Q
Z	G	B	G	R	U	F	C	M
S	A	P	P	H	I	R	A	W
I	H	D	C	C	O	T	Y	H

SAPPHIRA   CHRIST   APOSTLES
CHURCH   TRUTH   GIFT
           LIED

T is for Thomas

T T T T T T

Thomas Thomas

Thomas was a

disciple of Jesus.

FILL IN THE BLANKS
T is for Thomas

1. Thomas was one of the _____ chosen to share the good news about Jesus to the Jews.

2. After Jesus had been crucified, he rose on the _____ day of the week, _____.

3. Thomas wanted to _____ the prints in Jesus' hand and where they pierced him in his _____.

4. When Jesus appeared again to his disciples, _____ was there.

5. When _____ touched Jesus, he believed that Jesus had _____ from the dead.

6. Faith is _____ God even when we cannot _____ what he is doing or what is happening.

Please list five things you know about faith.

word search

```
E I B S U C E D S
F Z E X M R Y V A
A F L A N U J X M
I P I E R C E D O
T Q E T J I S Z H
H P V T A F U U T
C M E G O Y S W O
S E L P I C S I D
```

THOMAS PIERCED CRUCIFY
DISCIPLES FAITH BELIEVE
  JESUS

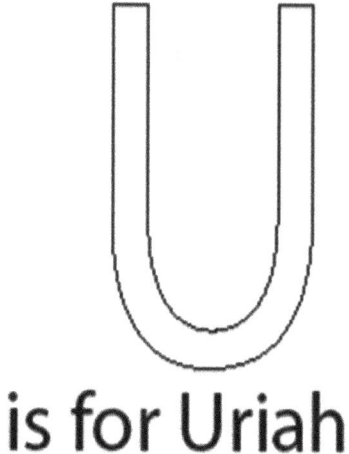
is for Uriah

Uu Uu Uu Uu Uu

Uriah Uriah Uriah

Uriah died serving

King David

FILL IN THE BLANKS
U is for Uriah

1. Uriah was a _____ in King David's army.

2. Uriah believed in King David's _____.

3. Uriah was married to a woman named _____.

4. King David took Bathsheba as if she were his _____.

5. Uriah was so committed to _____ in the battle with the king's soldiers Uriah did not know King _____ had placed him on the front line to be killed.

6. As a result of his _____ to King David, he died serving King David.

In two paragraphs, write what lessons you may have learned from this story.

word search

T	H	G	I	L	A	L	D	B
Y	L	U	Q	A	S	M	A	Z
T	B	R	F	Y	S	T	V	O
D	E	I	K	O	T	A	I	N
W	Y	A	R	L	M	F	D	P
K	J	H	E	Q	O	B	E	I
L	S	O	L	D	I	E	R	S
K	I	L	L	E	D	A	H	I

URIAH   BATTLE   LOYAL
DAVID   KILLED   LIGHT
        SOLDIERS

V is for Vashti

Vv Vv Vv Vv Vv

Vashti Vashti

Vashti refused to

go to the king's

party.

TRUE OR FALSE
V is for Vashti

_____ 1. Queen Vashti took a very bold stand against her husband King Xerxes and refused to attend his banquet.

_____ 2. The Bible states that Queen Vashti was a very beautiful woman and did not have to attend the King's party because she was the Queen.

_____ 3. There was no drinking at the banquet.

_____ 4. The significance of this story is two-fold in that Queen Vashti refused to be embarrassed by the king and by her refusal she opened the door for Esther to become Queen and save her people, the Jews, from destruction.

In two paragraphs, write what lessons you may have learned from this story.

word search

```
E X R S E E U L Q
T Z L M H N Y K I
E N A G A I N S T
U T S A O U W P H
Q L U G R R D Z S
N N F D K W O Y A
A K E E W A A X V
B J R X E R X E S
```

VASHTI BANQUET AGAINST
XERXES DRUNK   WEEK
        REFUSAL

W is for Woman @ the well

Ww Ww Ww Ww

woman at the well

The woman at the

well was from

Samaria.

FILL IN THE BLANKS
W is for woman at the well

1. Jews and _____ did not hang out together. This is because of some bad history that occurred when Jews were slaves in Babylonia.

2. Jesus was on his way back to _____ and he had to pass through a town in Samaria named _____.

3. A Samaritan woman came to draw _____ and Jesus asked her for a drink.

4. Jesus told the Samaritan woman that the water he could give her would be _____ _____ and that she would never thirst again.

Complete the picture. Draw and color the woman beneath the pitcher.

word search

```
A R E T A W U N S
W E X P A O D A Y
O B J O F M M Y C
M D G H N A V E H
D A S W R N M L A
C R R I V K I L R
Z G A L I L E E F
A E T W U Z Y W A
```

WOMAN   GALILEE   WELL
SYCHAR DRAW   SAMARIA
        WATER

X is for Xerxes

Xx Xx Xx Xx Xx Xx Xx

Xerxes Xerxes

King Xerxes made

Esther his queen.

TRUE OR FALSE
X is for Xerxes

_____ 1. King Xerxes was a very powerful king.

_____ 2. The party and the banquet lasted for two years.

_____ 3. He displayed all his wealth and his riches to his friends.

_____ 4. When Queen Esther refused to be put on display in front of the king and his friends, he ultimately choose Queen Vashti to be the next queen.

_____ 5. God used Xerxes, he chose Esther to be queen to save her people, the Jews, from being destroyed.

Create an invitation that the King could send out to invite his royal subjects to his party.

word search

```
X E R X E S G H V
E D A F Q D C G R
C E B R I N D I A
S L D I K E F Q Z
N U E C O I H Z W
F R W H O R S Y K
P O W E R F U L J
U C V S N B C X P
```

XERXES CUSH   FRIENDS
INDIA   RICHES POWERFUL
        RULED

Y
is for Yahweh

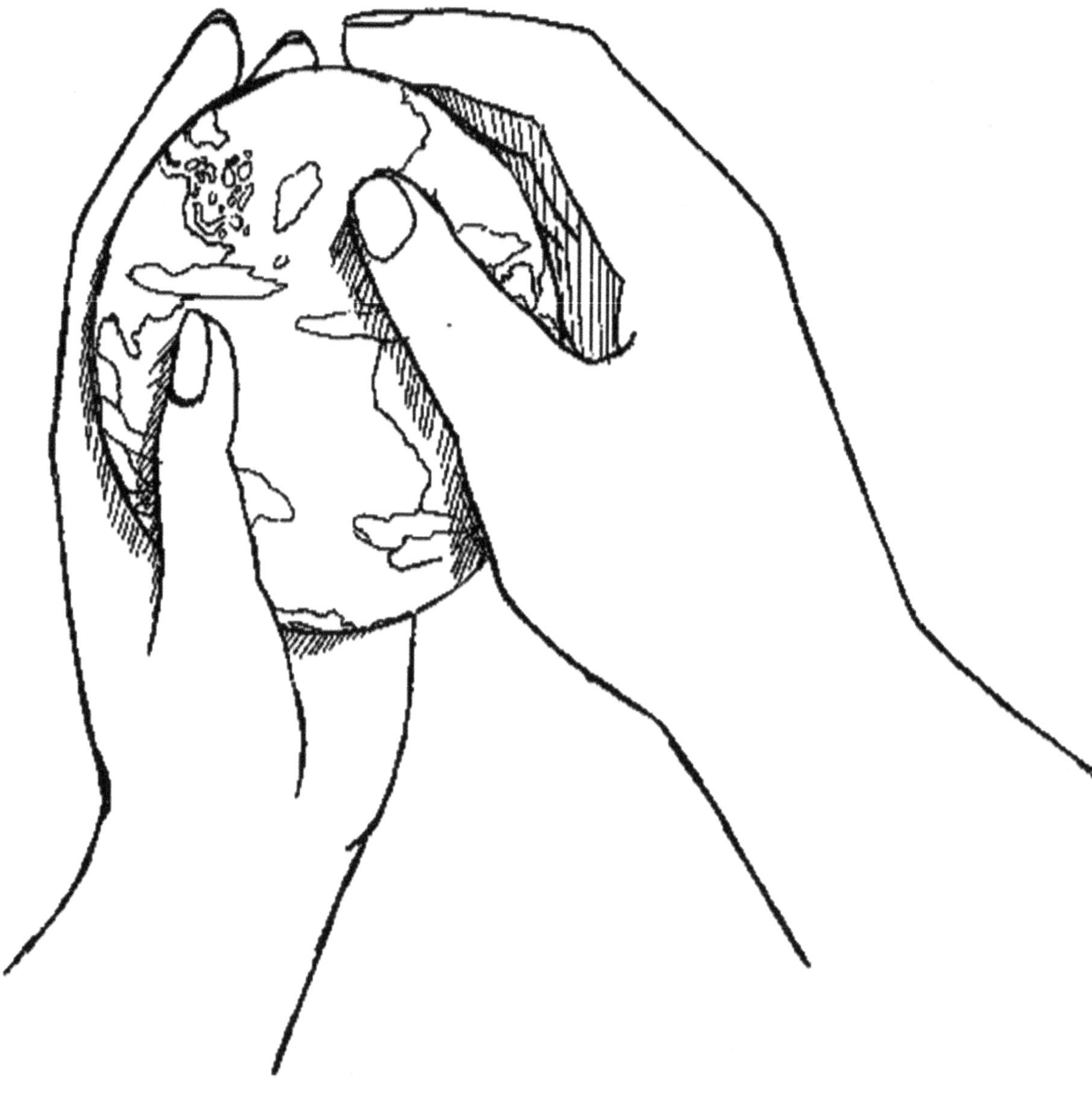

Yy Yy Yy Yy Yy Yy

Yahweh Yahweh

Yahweh has the

whole world in His

hands.

FILL IN THE BLANKS
Y is for Yahweh

1. In the beginning God created the _____ and the _____.

2. In _____ chapter 1, the Bible tells about all the beautiful things that God created.

3. On the sixth day, _____, _____, and the _____ _____ decided to make man in his own image.

4. John begins his book in the Bible telling us that _____ was with God in the beginning of time and that God sent his only begotten Son to save the world from their sins (John 3:16).

5. At the end of time, God, Jesus, and the Holy Spirit will come back to get those who have _____ and _____ what God has told them to do.

Write a letter to God about how beautiful you think His creation is.

word search

```
C A H Y H T R A E
R Z A N E W C X K
E Q V Y A H W E H
A U O M V L B O Y
T S H O E F L M V
E X E R N Y Z W U
D H J P S G A B C
S P I R I T O Q H
```

YAHWEH   EARTH   JEHOVAH
HEAVENS   HOLY   CREATED
          SPIRIT

Z
is for Zacchaeus

Z Z Z Z Z Z Z Z

Zacchaeus Zacchaeus

Zacchaeus wanted

to see Jesus.

TRUE OR FALSE
Z is for Zacchaeus

_____ 1. Zacchaeus was a tax collector and he was very tall.

_____ 2. People didn't like the idea of having to give their money to Zacchaeus to pay their taxes.

_____ 3. Because he was so short, he had to climb up a sycamore fig tree to see Jesus.

_____ 4. Zacchaeus threw a rock at Jesus so that he could see him in the tree.

_____ 5. Jesus told Zacchaeus that he would stay at his house that night.

Draw three men side by side: GOLIATH, DAVID, ZACCHAEUS

word search

```
J A Y E N O M O O
E M C H E A T E D
C D T E W G A B Y
Z A C C H A E U S
X U S K Z V R S U
V K J E R I C H O
N F I G T R E E T
R O T C E L L O C
```

ZACCHAEUS COLLECTOR JERICHO
FIG TREE   MONEY   CHEATED
           TAX

word search
PLAN OF SALVATION

```
D E Z I T P A B E B
A C V B R E P E N T
L U S S E F N O C L
R M G J K U I R S U
C O N Q K T W Z T F
Q P G M A J I T F H
X D H V Y H H I W T
B E L I E V E S X I
Z A E L D P A E V A
S O F N B A R T Y F
```

HEAR
BELIEVE

REPENT
CONFESS
BE BAPTIZED

FAITHFUL
SALVATION

Bible Phonics Name Song

"A" is for Adam
"B" is for Baal
"C" is for Cain
"D" is for Devil
"E" is for Enoch
"F" is for Festus
"G" is for Goliath
"H" is for Hagar
"I" is for Isaac
"J" is for Jacob
"K" is for the Kenites
"L" is for Lazarus
"M" is for Moses
"N" is for Noah
"O" is for Obadiah
"P" is for Paul
"Q" is for Queen Esther
"R" is for Rebekah
"S" is for Sapphira
"T" is for Thomas
"U" is for Uriah
"V" is for Vashti
"W" is for Woman at the Well
"X" is for Xerxes
"Y" is for Yahweh
"Z" is for Zacchaeus

You made it to the end now have a good day.

READERS

Aa, Aa, Adam Aa, Aa, Adam

Genesis 1

1 Adam was the first man that God created. He created Adam on the sixth day of creating the world.

2 God made Adam out of the dust of the ground. Isn't that great? No one can create another human being.

3 We can find the story of Adam in the book of Genesis, the first chapter. This is the first book in the Old Testament and the first book in the Bible.

4 Before God created Adam, he made the sky, vegetables, plants, trees, lights, sun, moon, animals and all living creatures.

5 God was very busy creating a beautiful world for us to live in. After God created a man and a woman, he was pleased with his work.

6 He rested on the seventh day.

Bb, Bb Baal   Bb, Bb Baal

1 Kings 18

1 This story talks about a prophet and a king.

2 The prophet's name is Elijah and the king's name is Ahab.

3 Elijah told King Ahab that the living God was greater than their god Baal.

4 King Ahab wanted to test what the prophet of God said.

5 So his 450 prophets killed a bull. They were to call on their god and their god was to answer putting fire under the bull.

6 Elijah also killed a bull and put no fire under it.

7 When the 450 prophets of Baal called out to their god, he never answered.

8 When Elijah called out to his God, he answered. God sent fire and burned up everything.

9 Can we count on God to answer our prayers?

10 We can always count on God to hear and answer our prayers because he loves and cares for us.

Cc, Cc, Cain Cc, Cc, Cain

Genesis 4:1-10

1 In the first family, there were problems.

2 It was time to make an offering to God.

3 Abel made an acceptable offering to God and Cain did not.

4 Cain got so angry that he killed his brother.

5 That made God so sad. Should we ever get that angry?

6 God sent Cain away for what he did.

7 He was very sad that Cain had sinned against Him and against his brother.

Dd, Dd, Devil Dd, Dd, Devil

Genesis 3:1-6

1 With the first <u>man</u> and <u>woman</u>, God gave them rules to obey.

2 <u>They</u> could eat of any tree in the <u>Garden of Eden</u> except the tree that was in the middle of the garden.

3 The <u>devil</u> talked them into eating from the tree that <u>God</u> told them not to.

4 <u>God</u> told them that if they ate from that tree, they would <u>die</u>.

The <u>devil</u> told them that they would ***not*** die.

5 That is not what <u>God</u> told them to do.

6 Because of their disobedience, <u>Adam</u> and <u>Eve</u> were punished by <u>God</u>.

7 Although <u>God</u> had to teach <u>Adam</u> and <u>Eve</u> a lesson, he still loved them.

8 Wouldn't you rather please <u>God</u> than make Him sad?

Ee, Ee, Enoch Ee, Ee, Enoch

Genesis 5:21-24

1 This story comes from the book of Genesis, the first book in the <u>Bible</u>.

2 The <u>Bible</u> tells us about all the wonderful things of <u>God</u>.

3 In our lesson, the <u>Bible</u> tells us that <u>Enoch</u> walked with <u>God</u>.

4 He did <u>not</u> die, for <u>God</u> took him.

5 <u>His</u> father, Jared, died at the age of <u>962</u>.

6 <u>His</u> son, Methuselah, died at the age of <u>969</u>.

7 God took <u>Enoch</u> when he was <u>365</u> years old.

Ff, Ff, Festus Ff, Ff, Festus

Acts 25: 21-24

1 In Acts 25, Festus was a member of the Roman government.

2 He had the authority to get Paul in trouble with the law.

3 This means that Paul could have gotten in trouble with the government.

4 But it was God working through Festus to allow Paul to speak about God to him.

5 God did not allow the Jewish leaders to take Paul to Jerusalem because they wanted to kill him.

6 It does not matter what people say, God can and will always take care of you (I Peter 5: 07).

8 We should always want to obey God because He loves us so Much.

Gg, Gg, Goliath Gg, Gg, Goliath

1 Samuel 17

1 In the book of 1 Samuel chapter 17, God's people are being teased by the Philistine army.

2 Jesse, David's father, had three sons who fought with Israel (the army of God).

3 Jesse sent David to take them food and to check on them.

4 While David was doing that, he saw Goliath teasing the armies of God.

5 Now Goliath was a giant (bigger than normal men), he stood nine feet tall.

6 He also wore lots of armor to protect himself.

7 David was the youngest of Jesse's sons but David was a strong and brave young man.

8 He destroyed a bear and a lion with the help of God because those animals attacked his sheep.

9 After David said what he could do to Goliath, Saul sent David to fight him.

10 David with the help of God killed Goliath with a sling and a smooth stone.

Hh, Hh, Hagar Hh, Hh, Hagar

Genesis 16

1 In Genesis 16, Sarai (Abraham's wife) had not had any children.

2 God had promised that Abraham would have a Big <u>family</u>. But Sarai still had not had any children.

3 <u>She</u> decided to help <u>God</u>.

4 Sarai had a handmaiden named <u>Hagar</u>.

5 Sarai told her husband <u>Abraham</u> to have a child with <u>Hagar</u>.

6 Abraham did as his wife asked of him.

7 When Hagar became pregnant, <u>she</u> despised Sarai because <u>she</u> could not have children.

8 Sarai mistreated <u>Hagar</u> and <u>Hagar</u> and her son Ishmael ran away.

9 God sent an angel to bring <u>Hagar</u> back <u>home</u>.

10 God promised that <u>Hagar's</u> son would be a mighty nation.

11 Abram was eighty-six years old when his son with <u>Hagar</u> named Ishmael was born.

12 Remember <u>God</u> sees you. His eyes see everything that we do.

Ii, Ii, Isaac, Ii, Ii, Isaac

Genesis 21 and 22

1 In Genesis 21, Sarah (Abraham's wife) had not had any children.

2 God had promised that Abraham would have a Big family.

3 Sarah (Genesis 22) became pregnant after a long time and had a son.

4 When Sarah had a son, Abraham named him Isaac.

5 Abraham was a hundred years old when Isaac was born.

6 He was the son that God had promised Abraham and Sarah.

7 God tested Abraham by telling Abraham to sacrifice his only son as a burnt offering. Abraham obeyed God.

8 God provided a ram instead of letting Abraham kill his son for the sacrifice.

9 God knew then that Abraham trusted and believed God.

Jj, Jj, Jacob Jj, Jj, Jacob

Genesis 25 and 27

1 In Genesis 25 and Genesis 27, the Bible talks about Jacob and his family.

2 Jacob father's name was Isaac.

3 Isaac was the son of Abraham and Sarah.

4 Isaac grows up and marries a woman named Rebekah. Isaac and Rebekah have twin sons, named Esau and Jacob.

5 Esau's skin was hairy, and Jacob's skin was smooth (Gen. 27:11).

6 While Rebekah was pregnant, it was foretold that the oldest son would serve the younger son (Gen. 25: 25).

7 God wanted Jesus to come through the family line of Jacob and God set his plan in action.

8 Remember, we are not as smart as God. God always knows how to make his plans work.

Kk, Kk, Kenites   Kk, Kk, Kenites

Judges 1:16 and 1 Samuel 15:6

1 In Judges 1:16, the Bible states that Moses' father-in-law, Jethro, was a Kenite.

2 Jethro was a shepherd and priest who lived in the land of Midian.

3 The Kenites journeyed with the Israelites to the land of Canaan.

4 The Kenites also showed kindness to the Israelites when they came out of Egypt (I Samuel 15:06).

5 King Saul did not want to destroy the Kenites with the Amalekites who lived in the city of Amalek.

6 Historically, the Kenites were nomadic, meaning that they traveled around.

7 The Kenites also invented working with bronze, iron, playing musical instruments, and creating art.

8 The Kenites also were a part of God's plan.

9 We are also a part of God's plan.

10 We should learn to follow God's plan just the way that God tells us to.

Ll, Ll, Lazarus Ll, Ll, Lazarus

John 11: 1-11

1 Today's story comes from the book of John in the New Testament.

2 Lazarus had two sisters, Mary and Martha. They were close friends to Jesus.

3 They were the kind of friends that could sit down, eat and hang out together.

4 Mary and Martha's brother got real sick and died.

5 Lazarus died and was buried four days before Jesus got back to Bethany where he lived.

6 Yes, Mary and Martha were very sad because their brother Lazarus had died.

7 Jesus brought Lazarus back to life.

9 God is Able to do whatever we believe that he can do.

Mm, Mm, Moses Mm, Mm, Moses

Exodus 1:15-2:1-10

1 In Exodus 1:15 -2:1-10, we read about the birth of Moses.

2 God had a very special job for Moses to do.

3 When Moses' mother gave birth to him, she hid him in an ark in the river to keep him from being killed.

4 His sister watched him from afar off.

5 Pharaoh's daughter found him and raised Moses as her own son.

6 Moses' mother took care of him while Pharaoh's daughter raised him.

7 This was part of God's plan to prepare him to save his people from slavery.

8 Moses did exactly what God wanted him to do.

9 We must be obedient to God, too.

10 God loves us just as he loved Moses and the Israelite people.

Nn, Nn, Noah, Nn, Nn, Noah

Genesis 7:1-24

1 In Genesis 7:1-24, we read about <u>Noah</u> and the ark.

2 God was <u>sad</u> that he made man. <u>God</u> decided to destroy man.

3 He told <u>Noah</u> to build an <u>ark</u>. This <u>ark</u> was special.

4 This <u>ark</u> was going to withstand a flood that would last <u>forty</u> days.

5 It was going to <u>rain</u> for forty days.

6 It began to <u>rain</u> and <u>rain</u> and <u>rain</u>.

7 God put <u>Noah</u>, his wife, his three sons and their wives and all the <u>animals</u> in the ark.

8 God saved <u>Noah</u> and his family because <u>Noah</u> was obedient to God.

9 God takes cares of those <u>who</u> are obedient to Him.

Oo, Oo, Obadiah, Oo, Oo, Obadiah

1 Kings 18:1-4

1 Obadiah worked for King Ahab, but Obadiah believed in God.

2 King Ahab ruled over Israel and he was an evil king.

3 He married Jezebel and they worshipped Baal.

4 Jezebel killed prophets who believed in God.

5 Obadiah took a hundred (100) prophets and hid them in two caves and took care of them.

6 The Bible says in 1Kings 18:4 that Obadiah fed them bread and water.

7 Although, his boss, King Ahab did not believe in God, Obadiah believed in God.

8 He did what was right in spite of how his boss acted.

9 We should always do what God wants us to do no matter what others say.

Pp, Pp, Paul, Pp, Pp, Paul

Acts 9:1-19

1 <u>Saul</u> met Jesus on the Damascus Road.

2 <u>Saul</u> was on his way to Damascus to hurt <u>Christians</u>, but Jesus stopped him on his <u>way</u>.

3 Jesus asked <u>Saul</u>, <u>Saul</u> "why do you persecute me?"

4 <u>Paul</u> had a repentant (changed) heart and decided to <u>obey</u> Jesus.

5 God sent <u>Paul</u> to Ananias' home and Ananias taught him what to do to become a <u>Christian</u>.

6 In verse 18, <u>Paul</u> was baptized for the remission of his <u>sins</u> and became a <u>Christian</u>.

Qq, Qq, Queen Esther, Qq, Qq, Queen Esther

Esther

1 <u>Esther</u> was a <u>beautiful</u> <u>queen</u>.

2 Esther was chosen to be the queen after Queen Vashti refused to obey King Ahasuerus' cruel rules.

3 There was an evil <u>man</u> who worked for the King Ahasuerus named Haman.

4 He wanted to destroy all the <u>Jews</u> in the kingdom.

5 Haman's plan to destroy God's people actually ending up destroying him and his <u>family</u>.

6 Because <u>Esther</u> was a Jew, God allowed <u>Esther</u> to talk to the king to <u>save</u> her people.

7 God used Haman's evil plan to show how strong and mighty He Really is.

8 God placed <u>Esther</u> in the position to save her people from destruction.

Rr, Rr, Rebekah Rr, Rr, Rebekah

Genesis 27

1 Rebekah was married to Isaac, Abraham's son.

2 They had twin sons. The oldest of their children was named Esau and their youngest son was named Jacob.

3 God promised to bless Isaac because Abraham had done what God asked him to do.

4 God kept his promise. Isaac and Rebekah became very, very rich.

5 God always keeps his promises. But there were problems in the family.

6 Rebekah loved Jacob and Isaac loved Esau.

7 Because Rebekah tricked Isaac, Jacob received Esau's blessing.

8 It was God's plan for Jacob to become great but it was not right for Rebekah to trick her husband Isaac.

9 We should always wait for God instead of trying to do things our way. God will always work things out for our good.

Ss, Ss, Sapphira Ss, Ss, Sapphira

Acts 4: 32-37; 5: 1-11

1 There was a man and a woman who were members of the <u>church</u> named Ananias and <u>Sapphira</u>.

2 The people would bring their <u>gifts</u> to the apostles to share with others.

3 Ananias lied and told the apostle Peter that this was all the money for the land that he and his wife collected. This was not the <u>truth</u>.

4 Peter told <u>him</u> that this was not the <u>truth</u> and Ananias died at that moment.

5 About three hours later, Sapphira walked in and said the same thing that her husband said.

6 <u>She</u> died too.

7 Ananias and <u>Sapphira</u> lied to God.

8 <u>It</u> is never good to <u>lie</u> to God because God already knows what you are thinking.

9 <u>They</u> should have told the truth. Telling the truth is always better than lying.

10 When we tell the truth, we can trust that God will help us to bear our consequences.

Tt, Tt, Thomas Tt, Tt, Thomas

John 20: 24-29

1 <u>Thomas</u> was one of the disciples chosen to share the <u>good</u> news about <u>Jesus</u> to the Jews.

2 After Jesus had been crucified, he <u>rose</u> on the <u>first</u> <u>day</u> of the week, <u>Sunday</u>.

3 <u>Thomas</u> was not there. He did not believe.

4 <u>Thomas</u> wanted to touch the prints in <u>Jesus'</u> hand and where they pierced him in his side.

5 When Jesus appeared again to his disciples, <u>Thomas</u> was there.

6 He had a chance to touch Jesus and then he believed that Jesus had risen from the dead.

7 Faith is believing God even when we cannot see what he is doing or what is happening.

Uu, Uu, Uriah Uu, Uu, Uriah

2 Samuel 11:1-27

1 Uriah was a soldier in King David's army.

2 He was a good soldier, too. He cared so much about King David and his army.

3 He believed in David's God, as well. His name meant, "God is my light".

4 Uriah was married to a woman named Bathsheba.

5 Uriah's wife, Bathsheba was very pretty.

6 King David decided that he would take her like she was his wife.

7 Uriah was so committed to fighting in the battle with the king's soldiers that he did not know what King David had done.

8 As a result of his loyalty to King David, he died serving King David.

Vv, Vv, Vashti Vv, Vv, Vashti

Esther 1:10-12; 19

1 Queen <u>Vashti</u> took a very bold stand against her husband King Xerxes.

2 King Xerxes decided to give a <u>week</u> long <u>banquet</u> for all his nobles and officials.

3 He sent for the queen on the seventh day of his banquet.

4 He wanted her to wear <u>her</u> royal crown and prance around so that everyone could see how beautiful she was.

5 The Bible says that Queen <u>Vashti</u> was a very <u>beautiful</u> woman.

6 Queen <u>Vashti</u> said, emphatically NO. This was very bold on <u>her</u> part because you don't ever say no the king.

7 But <u>she</u> refused to be disgraced in front of the drunk king and his drunk friends.

8 God used Queen Vashti to put Esther in <u>her</u> place to be the queen and save <u>her</u> people.

Ww, Ww, Woman at the Well, Ww, Ww

John 4:1-42

1 Jews and Samaritans did not hang out together.

2 While Jesus was on his <u>way</u> back to Galilee, he had to pass through a town in Samaria named Sychar.

3 He stopped at Jacob's well because he was tired.

3 Later a <u>Samaritan</u> <u>woman</u> came to draw water and Jesus asked her for a drink.

4 Jesus told this <u>woman</u> all about herself. She was so thrilled that she ran into town and told everybody what Jesus said about her.

5 Jesus offered the <u>Samaritan</u> <u>woman</u> "living water".

6 Many <u>Samaritans</u> became believers (vs. 39) after they listened to Jesus.

7 Jesus showed the <u>Samaritan</u> <u>woman</u> that it didn't matter what she looked like or what her background was, it was only important that she Believe.

8 It is important, <u>boys</u> and <u>girls</u>, that you believe and obey what Jesus tells us to do.

Xx, Xx, Xerxes, Xx, Xx

Esther 1-2

1 King Xerxes was a very powerful king.

2 He ruled over 127 provinces or areas from India to Cush.

3 King Xerxes decided to give a party for all the people who worked for him.

4 The party lasted for 180 days and then he decided to give a banquet for seven days.

5 He showed all his wealth and his riches to his friends.

6 He also wanted to display his beautiful queen, Vashti.

7 When Queen Vashti refused to be put on display in front of the king and his friends, he choose Esther to be the next queen.

8 God used Xerxes, to choose Esther to be queen to save her people, the Jews, from being destroyed.

Yy, Yy, Yahweh, Yy, Yy, Yahweh
Genesis 1:01;26; John 1:1-5; Revelation 22:17-21

1. In the <u>beginning</u> God created the <u>heavens</u> and the <u>earth</u>.

2. In Genesis chapter 1, the Bible tells us about all the beautiful things that <u>God</u> created.

3. On the <u>sixth</u> day, <u>God</u>, <u>Jesus</u>, and the <u>Holy</u> <u>Spirit</u> decided to make man in his own image.

4. John began his book in the Bible telling us that God sent his only begotten Son to save the world from their sins (John 3:16).

5. At the end of time, Jesus will come back to get those who have believed and obeyed what God has told them to do.

6. God tells us what he wants us to do in the Bible.

7. <u>Yahweh</u> means <u>Jehovah</u>. <u>Jehovah</u> is the name that can only be given to God. Our God is omnipotent, omniscient, and omnipresent.

8. <u>Jehovah</u> <u>God</u> is all-powerful, all-knowing, and everywhere. He is Everything!

Zz, Zz, Zacchaeus, Zz, Zz, Zacchaeus

Luke 19: 1-10

1 Zacchaeus was a tax collector and he was very short.

2 Being a tax collector meant that he collected money (taxes) that were owed to the Roman government.

3 People didn't like the idea of having to give their money to Zacchaeus.

4 One day when Jesus was passing through Jericho, Zacchaeus wanted to see him.

5 Because he was so short, he had to climb up a sycamore tree to see Jesus.

6 Jesus is so smart that when he got to the tree, he looked up and saw Zacchaeus.

7 Jesus told Zacchaeus that he would stay at his house that night.

8 Because of Jesus, Zacchaeus decided not to cheat anyone and to help others.

9 Isn't it amazing to see what God can do in all of our lives?

ANSWER SHEET FOR THE WORKSHEETS

A is for Adam
Adam
sixth (6th)
dust
man, woman, pleased
seventh (7th)

B is for Baal
eighteen (18)
prophets
Ahab, greater
god, god
prophets, Elijah

C is for Cain
acceptable
angry
killed
Cain
brother

D is for Devil
Garden of Eden
devil (snake or serpent)
tree, die
disobedience, Eve
Adam, Eve

E is for Enoch
False
True
True
False
False
True

F is for Festus
government
Paul, God
Jewish, Jerusalem

always, I Peter
God

G is for Goliath
True
True
True
False
False

H is for Hagar
False
True
True
False
True

I is for Isaac
True
True
True
False
True

J is for Jacob
Isaac
Abraham
Rebekah
Jacob, Esau
hairy, smooth

K is for Kenite
False
True
True
False
True
True

L is for Lazarus
John
Mary, Martha
sick, died
Lazarus
Jesus
God

M is for Moses
True
True
False
False
True
True

N is for Noah
False
False
False
True
True
True

O is for Obadiah
Ahab
evil
Jezebel, Baal
Jezebel, caves
bread, water

P is for Paul
True
False
True
True
False
True

Q is for Queen
Queen
Vashti
Haman
Jews
him, family
Esther, save

R is for Rebekah
True
False
False
True
True
False

S is for Sapphira
True
True
True
True
True

T is for Thomas
Disciples
first (1st), Sunday
touch, side
Thomas
Thomas, risen
believing, see

U is for Uriah
soldier
God
Bathsheba
wife
fighting, David
loyalty

V is for Vashti
True
False
False
True

W is for woman at the well
Samaritans
Galilee, Sychar
water
living water

X is for Xerxes
True
False
True
False
True

Y is for Yahweh
Heavens, earth
Genesis
God, Jesus, Holy Spirit
Jesus
believed, obey

Z is for Zacchaeus
False
True
True
False
True

Unscramble Activities
D is for Devil
Adam
Lived
Disobedience
Garden
Woman
Loved

F is for Festus
Jewish
Festus
Leaders
God
Peter
Acts

R is for Rebekah
Esau
Jacob
Abraham
Rebekah
Isaac
God

Cross Word
O is for Obadiah
Across
1 Obadiah
2 Jezebel
3 Prophets
4 Bread
Down
1 Worshipped
2 Ahab
3 Evil
4 Storm

S is for Sapphira
Across
1 Sapphira
2 gifts
3 lied
4 truth
Down
1 die
2 Apostle
3 Ananias
4 Church

A is for Adam
word search

C	Z	U	G	H	L	M	A	N
R	E	S	T	E	D	O	T	O
E	W	D	P	F	C	O	A	Q
A	N	S	C	H	Z	N	M	D
T	B	V	M	T	N	L	R	M
I	Q	K	E	R	J	I	A	A
O	Y	W	M	A	E	R	O	D
N	E	V	A	E	H	X	B	A

ADAM   HEAVEN   RESTED
MOON   EARTH   CREATION
MAN

D is for Devil
word search

DEVIL   RULES   EVE
OBEY   EDEN   DIE
       WOMAN

G is for Goliath
word search

GOLIATH   SLING   JESSE
ARMY   DAVID   GIANT
       ARMOR

B is for Baal
word search

B	D	E	L	I	J	A	H	Q
E	H	T	U	S	N	F	Z	S
B	G	W	I	K	K	I	N	G
D	Z	Q	S	J	I	R	U	O
A	C	M	R	W	N	E	X	R
H	P	O	A	R	M	K	L	J
A	H	V	E	X	G	F	C	T
B	A	A	L	P	G	O	D	V

BAAL   AHAB   ISRAEL
ELIJAH   GOD   KING
       FIRE

E is for Enoch
word search

ENOCH   JARED   BIBLE
WALKED   SON   AGE
       GENESIS

H is for Hagar
word search

HAGAR   FAMILY   WIFE
SARAI   HUSBAND   ISHMAEL
       HANDMAID

C is for Cain
word search

G	O	F	F	E	R	I	N	G
F	H	B	N	O	A	Z	O	Y
M	E	R	M	N	Q	L	J	S
P	L	O	A	N	G	R	Y	I
N	B	T	V	D	C	S	D	N
I	W	H	R	Q	U	B	X	N
A	B	E	L	S	A	K	W	E
C	Z	R	K	I	L	L	E	D

CAIN   OFFERING   BROTHER
ABEL   ANGRY   SINNED
       KILLED

F is for Festus
word search

F	E	S	T	U	S	O	O	L
A	G	H	A	N	M	J	R	A
C	P	Z	X	V	W	E	Y	W
G	A	U	X	W	W	W	Z	A
A	U	T	H	O	R	I	T	Y
C	L	P	V	L	T	S	Y	U
T	B	E	E	L	F	H	M	P
S	I	O	J	A	K	L	Q	C

FESTUS   PAUL   ALLOW
ACTS   LAW   JEWISH
       AUTHORITY

I is for Isaac
word search

ISAAC   ABRAHAM   TRUST
PROMISE   BURNT   RAM
       SACRIFICE

J is for Jacob
word search

JACOB TWINS OLDEST
ESAU SKIN SOUP
HAIRY

M is for Moses
word search

MOSES PHARAOH SAVE
MOTHER EXODUS SLAVERY
DAUGHTER

P is for Paul
word search

PAUL CHRISTIAN BAPTIZED
DAMASCUS PERSECUTE CHANGE
ANANIAS

K is for Kenites
word search

KENITES PRIEST NOMADIC
JETHRO EGYPT BRONZE
AMALEK

N is for Noah
word search

NOAH BUILD ANIMALS
ARK FLOOD RAIN
FORTY

Q is for Queen
word search

QUEEN VASHTI HAMAN
BEAUTIFUL ESTHER REFUSED
AHASUERUS

L is for Lazarus
word search

LAZARUS MARY SISTER
JOHN MARTHA BURIED
BETHANY

O is for Obadiah
word search

OBADIAH FERTILITY STORM
EVIL BREAD BELIEVE
WORSHIP

R is for Rebekah
word search

REBEKAH GOD LOVE
TRICKED ESAU PROMISE
ISAAC

S is for Sapphira
word search

SAPPHIRA CHRIST APOSTLES
CHURCH TRUTH GIFT
         LIED

V is for Vashti
word search

VASHTI   BANQUET AGAINST
XERXES   DRUNK   WEEK
         REFUSAL

Y is for Yahweh
word search

YAHWEH   EARTH   JEHOVAH
HEAVENS HOLY   CREATED
         SPIRIT

T is for Thomas
word search

THOMAS   PIERCED CRUCIFY
DISCIPLES FAITH   BELIEVE
           JESUS

W is for Woman at the Well
word search

WOMAN   GALILEE WELL
SYCHAR DRAW   SAMARIA
        WATER

Z is for Zacchaeus
word search

ZACCHAEUS COLLECTOR JERICHO
FIG TREE   MONEY   CHEATED
           TAX

U is for Uriah
word search

URIAH BATTLE   LOYAL
DAVID KILLED   LIGHT
       SOLDIERS

X is for Xerxes
word search

XERXES CUSH   FRIENDS
INDIA   RICHES POWERFUL
        RULED

The Plan of Salvation
word search
PLAN OF SALVATION

HEAR   REPENT   FAITHFUL
BELIEVE CONFESS   SALVATION
         BE BAPTIZED

Copy and cut sentence strips and attach together to write Bible Verses:

Copy and cut sentence strips and attach together to write Bible Verses:

Copy and cut sentence strips and attach together to write Bible Verses:

References

Dyslexia Intervention Program Manuel. Houston, TX: Region 4 ESC, Reading/La Services.

Joyce, B., Weil, M., & Calhoun, E. (2004). Models of Teaching (7th ed.). Boston, MA: Pearson Education.

Pressley, M. (2002). Reading instruction that works: The case for balanced teaching (2nded.). New York: The Guilford Press.

The Hebrew-Greek Key Word Study Bible. (2008). South Korea: AMG Publishers.

The Holy Bible, New International Version. (2011). SE. Grand Rapids, MI: Zondervan.

Reviews

Are you looking for a Fun and Interactive Way for your most precious possession to learn about God? The Bible Phonics Curriculum is a clever and practical model for teaching reading and writing, while learning about God's Wonderful Love. I love it because it enhances reading, speaking, listening, and writing skills enveloped in Bible stories.
--Veronica C.
Counselor and Bible School Teacher

What vision, diligence, thoughtfulness, and understanding. The creation of this collection of Bible stories, songs, and readers is truly a work of art to help the very young start their spiritual journey and strengthen the kingdom of God.
--James A.
Educator and Bible School Teacher

This curriculum is well designed to implement learning of the Bible. In addition to improving reading, writing, speaking and listening skills, the Bible Phonics Curriculum is family friendly and will change how our students interpret their world. This learning experience will create life-long learners and followers of Jesus.
--Urissa H.
Therapist, Counselor, and Bible School Teacher

DR. HALL'S BIO

Dr. Hall is a retired Visiting Instructor in the School of Communication at Texas Southern University. With a background in reading and speech communication, Dr. Hall has learned that reading is the fundamental skill that enhances all other disciplines. She has taught students for over twenty years in K-12 and college environments.

This curriculum was written with children in mind. Her objective is to teach reading skills and instill godly values in children's lives. This text will help children and facilitators know the power of the Almighty and develop long-life readers.

Dr. Hall has been married 31 years to James A. Hall. They have four children, six grandchildren and two great-grandchildren. Dr. Hall hopes that the Bible Phonics Curriculum rejuvenates reading for both the child and facilitator. Please enjoy and take this journey with me through God's word.

www.ingramcontent.com/pod-product-compliance
Lightning Source LLC
Chambersburg PA
CBHW061110070526
44583CB00027B/3250